The 1960s Segregated South:

Youth's Zeal and Aged Reflections

Robert W. Hoffert

Robert W. Hoffert

ISBN-13: 978-1-7321976-5-7
Library of Congress Control Number: 2020904278

Published by:
Jujapa Press, LLC
PO Box 269
Hansville, Wa 98340

Author and Cover images by: Alex Rodas

This book is dedicated to the past and to the future.

To those who suffered great injustices and gave so much in
behalf of justice.
"Some of them of recognized eminence,
others less known than they deserve to be,
and the ones to whom most of all is due,
those who toiled and suffered whom the world
had no opportunity of knowing."
(John Stuart Mill)

And to those to whom we entrust our future.
In my case, Jake, Reis, Roberta and Graham.
May they be guided by the simple wisdom
that the justice we provide and protect for others –
all others –
is the strongest foundation for the justice we seek for
ourselves.

Robert W. Hoffert

Table of Contents

Robert W. Hoffert

Foreward

The decision to write about my experiences in the South
from 1964 through 1968 brought me face to face with an
unanticipated quandary. How do I explain offering an
account that is not essentially about myself and that, other
than among my immediate loved ones, would spark little
interest about me or my story? Yes, it is about my
experiences, but it is a story that rightly belongs to others, to
their struggles, and to their accomplishments. Then I
remembered the rather unique first paragraph explanation
offered by John Stuart Mill to his <u>Autobiography</u>.
Presumptuous as it is, I decided that an edited rewriting of
Mill's paragraph would be the solution to my quandary.

Here it is.

"It seems proper that I should prefix to the following
biographical sketch of my experiences from 1964 to 1968 in
Florida, Georgia and Alabama, some mention of the
reasons which have made me think it desirable that I should
leave behind an account of so insignificant a life as mine. I
do not for a moment imagine that any part of what I have

to relate can be interesting to the general public as a narrative, or as some important account about myself. But I have thought that in an age in which matters of social justice, and its improvement, are the subject of attacks, disputes and relentless efforts, it may be useful that there should be records of experiences which were remarkable in setting the stage for many contemporary perspectives and engagements. It has also seemed to me that in an age of transition in opinions, there may be both interest and benefit in noting earlier phases in a struggle which is always pressing forward. But a motive which weighs more on me than either of these, is a desire to acknowledge debts to which my experiences and development owe to other persons; some of them of recognized eminence, others less known than they deserve to be, and the ones to whom most of all is due, those who toiled and suffered whom the world had no opportunity of knowing."

Mill, John Stuart. **Essential Works**, *"Autobiography",*
Bantam Books, New York, 1961

CHAPTER 1
Martin Luther King Day
2009

Maureen and I returned home from the Martin Luther King Day march here in Fort Collins. As we walked down College Avenue, we organized our day in preparation for tomorrow so we can watch President Obama's inaugural address. Immediately upon returning home, I found an email message from my Uncle Paul. His request stunned and touched me – "...please think back to a time four plus decades ago in Keysville, Georgia. I repeat please record your first-hand thoughts for us your family. Give us an insight of your feelings as well as what tomorrow's events mean to you." This startling request I felt compelled to honor.

I lived in the segregated South from June 1964 thru August 1965 and from August 1966 thru September 1968. For the most part, I have kept memories and thoughts from these experiences guarded deep inside me. Perhaps now I can dare to bring what I have cherished and protected into the light of a new day. The historic circumstances of our times, prodded by Uncle Paul's completely unexpected intimate request, have led me to give it a try.

As I said, I had two periods of experiences in the South during the 1960s that bracketed my final year of study at Yale. The first period was built around my June 1964 experiences in St. Augustine, Florida and my August 1964 through August 1965 work at Boggs Academy in Keysville, Georgia. From August 1966 thru September 1968 I worked at Alabama A & M University, Huntsville, Alabama.

Before I share my memories about my life in these settings, let me comment on why I have been so reluctant to share them throughout most of the last 50 years. I have felt the weight of two concerns – one a bit more practical and the other profoundly personal. My former concern was that honest, candid sharing might contribute to misunderstandings as much or even more than to understanding. For example, the academic performances of my students, overall, were poor and inadequate. Perhaps I underestimate people, but I know there are too many people who will hear me say that and use it to reinforce their prejudicial attitudes about the potential of my students. They have little or no appreciation for the circumstances - immediate, pervasive and long-term - that contributed directly and significantly to the quality of those students' academic performances. I am committed to do all I can never to fuel the poisonous perceptions that already have so harshly limited and damaged the growth and opportunities of millions of young Americans like those I knew at Boggs and Alabama A & M.

Perhaps we don't always consider why we may need secrets. Too often it's assumed that to keep a secret is to hide something, usually something that is sinister or a source of shame or inadequacy or failure. Like most others, I carry those kinds of secrets within me too. But I have other secrets. They are secrets that have nourished my life, given me strength and perspective, and grounded me in steadfast purposes. They, more than anything else in my life, give me a measure of self-worth and a sense of accomplishments worthy of the name. I have kept them secret because they are precious. I can't afford to have them tramped upon or trivialized by others. And I can't afford to cheapen them myself by using them instrumentally rather than protecting and honoring their intrinsic value.

So, why do I share now? I'm not sure. I do know two things. First, for several years I have felt organic changes within me that have permitted me, even encouraged me at

3

times, to share more – not all, just more. And my sense is that in doing so I have not damaged others or myself. I hope that perception is right. Second, even in writing this account, I will continue to protect secrets – not to deceive or mislead anyone, but to honor the inexpressible power of these experiences in my life. Socrates was right to call us to the pursuit of knowledge, but we should not forget how much we also need to protect the mysteries and fragile truths inherent in mortal life as well. Our efforts to bring light into the world will never illuminate every niche of our being and experiences.

In what follows, I hope to do two things – tell true stories and end with some personal reflections upon them. When I say "tell true stories," I don't mean TRUE stories in the absolute sense of religious or philosophical presumption. I mean the only kind of true stories one human can share with other humans – stories that are honest representations of what is remembered and believed to be accurate about those remembrances. They will not be the infallible account of God, but they will have the full integrity of Bob. Over the years, I have come to have less and less confidence in the specific details of my memories. I question myself more and more about specifics. I mention this to you not as an excuse or cover-up. Everything I will share with you I will share as the truth I know. However, you need to remember my limits, and the limits of each of us, as vessels of truth.

Robert W. Hoffert

CHAPTER 2
Yale
Spring of 1964

My route to St. Augustine relates more to my struggles with
faith than to the highways I drove in my 1956 Plymouth.
Between my boyhood and my 20th birthday, I was possessed
of both devout faith and disturbing doubts related to my
faith. On the one hand, I had no way to understand myself
except as a deeply committed Christian. On the other hand,
there were things a committed Christian was asked to
believe that made no sense to me and Christianity too often
manifested itself in ghoulishly unchristian ways. Amid this
turbulence, I came to a firm conclusion: my faith had to
relate to the transformation of my life and world, not just to
the salvation of my soul.

But that's a different story – one I will reflect on later.
Suffice it to say, in the fall of 1963 I decided that I could
not continue studying Christian theology at Yale. President
Kennedy's assassination transformed that from a decision
into an emotional imperative. Not knowing what to do but
wanting to do something that really mattered to me, I
applied for service in the Peace Corps. I was accepted and

assigned to work in Ethiopia. I was filled with excited anticipation. But when I told my parents in February of 1964, both were distressed but Dad's response was the more challenging. He said I had chosen to kill him because he had committed me to God's service in the Christian ministry. Within weeks he had another heart attack. I withdrew from the Peace Corps assignment. I was lost, distressed, worried, and angry.

Throughout my second year at Yale, I may have attended more chapel services than anyone else in my class. These were not acts of piety, but of defiance. I went to express subtle contempt and vigorous criticism. This pattern intensified following the loss of the Peace Corps option. I started to go to chapel services down on the old campus at Battell Chapel as well. Occasionally, I listened and was able to hear more than what I disrespected or wanted to discard. William Sloane Coffin was the chaplain and lived, as he spoke, a life committed to social justice. One April day following a service, I stopped at the bulletin board by the mailboxes in the basement of the chapel. Coffin had posted opportunities for our involvement.

Two of them changed my life. The Southern Christian Leadership Conference (SCLC) was looking for someone to come to Florida in June to help organize and produce a community newspaper for a planned desegregation campaign. The other was from the Board of National Missions of the United Presbyterian Church USA for a teacher/chaplain at Boggs Academy. That's how I got to St. Augustine in June and to Keysville in August, 1964.

In late May of 1964 I left white Quakertown to live in the black south. I soon discovered that I didn't have a fully authentic place in either one. My departure was tortured. I don't remember exactly what I told Mother and Dad, but I know it was not the whole story. About St. Augustine I focused on the community newspaper and about Boggs, initially, I only shared my work as a teacher. They were uneasy, probably suspicious. Their only comfort was that I wasn't leaving for Ethiopia.

Robert W. Hoffert

CHAPTER 3
St. Augustine, Florida
June 1964

I have no memory of entering St. Augustine or how I found
my way to the home of an elderly black woman with whom
I lived while there. I do have a totally romanticized image
of her. She was slight, gentle, humble, generous, strong,
and wise. Resistance, however she knew it, had always been
something quietly internal for her. That approach no longer
was sufficient. Even with her firm constitution and
compelling commitment, it clearly challenged her to have a
young white man living in her modest, two room home.
We came to have a measure of comfort with each other.
She told me on the day I left that opening up her home to
me helped her appreciate herself more. She didn't elaborate
and I didn't press.

I have few memories of my work on the newspaper.
Actually, it was more like a pamphlet or flyer. It was a
means to inform and mobilize the community about the
campaign. It was supposed to be my primary responsibility
and purpose for being in St. Augustine. But even before I
arrived, I knew it was my excuse for purposes that were

more compelling to me – The Campaign. The campaign was SCLC's (Southern Christian Leadership Conference) plan to reverse local laws requiring the segregation of public life and facilities in St. Augustine. For example, I was discouraged from attending the rallies and marches so that work on the newspaper would not be interrupted. I believe I honored that expectation the first night, but quickly decided it was a constraint I could not accept.

Rallies were held at night in the largest black church in the community – I'm quite positive it was a Baptist church, but, shamefully, I didn't pay attention. You could feel the community starting to come alive, to believe in itself, to recognize and trust its own efficacy. Near the middle of each night's rally there was a march from the church to the Slave Market and back to the church. I didn't march the first night I attended the rally. After that, I also marched. Over the years, there were times I thought I remembered the specific details of each night's march. I no longer trust those kinds of precise remembrances. I do trust several indelible memories, even if their specific sequences escape me.

To this day, I can feel the exhilaration and terror when we turned the corner leaving the black community on our way to the Slave Market. The tension was thicker than the humidity. We walked in pairs. We sang, but we could not respond or taunt. I was frightened, but I never felt more alive. Police, local and state, were everywhere. Immediately, I saw them differently than I had ever seen officers of the law before. They were threatening, not protecting, and they created danger, not a safe-haven. They looked at us with contempt – a perception I too readily reciprocated.

We were challenged mostly by young, white males. They were crude. Their passion had an eerie quality to it – a perverse mixture of a holy crusade and a sophomoric stag party. The hand-full of whites among the marchers seemed to be a unique focus of their attention and specific ire. At times, my mental experiences seemed to separate me from my physical experiences. It felt like a chorus of thousands screaming "white Nigger", even if it actually was just one acne-faced, redneck kid yelling it in my ear. Either way, it was real. Either way, its only purpose was to express complete and utter contempt.

Some of these juveniles had pried loose bricks used to pave paths in the Slave Market Park. They climbed trees, dropping and throwing them at us. During one of the marches, an elderly white woman who had been born in St. Augustine and had lived her entire life there was attacked. Whether by specific intent or not I don't know, but one of those bricks hit her on the head. She fell to the ground unconscious. Scores of policemen were near her. They stood unmoved. They were asked to assist; to get her to a doctor or hospital. They stood unmoved. My contempt deepened. Several black young men locked hands and carried her to the nearest hospital.

I believe it was the last night I marched, but am not certain. In any case, one hot night after we had returned to the church from the march, most of us stood in the street, delaying our return to the steamy sanctuary as long as possible. Unexpectedly, a car approached us from the one side. As it neared the church, there were screams as it sped through the crowd and disappeared. Two or three young white boys were in the car. They threw a burning liquid, directly hitting a young black girl. Experiences such as these rapidly seasoned my resolve and moral convictions. They may not have hardened my heart completely, but they created a steely determination to take on the challenges they presented.

On the third or fourth night, we all knew something special was waiting for us when we returned to the church from the march. Dr. Martin Luther King Jr. was going to be there to lead us into the next phase of the campaign. The church was filled way beyond its capacity. I stood along one of the sidewalls. I can't remember what he said or how he said it. I only know the intensity of his impact was unlike any previous experience in my nearly 24 years of life.

I do remember "The Plan" he presented to us. The next day, Dr. King and a handful of others will be arrested for violating St. Augustine's segregation laws. Each day after that 40 to 50 people will be similarly arrested. Although anyone arrested can be released easily for the misdemeanor charges that will be made against them, each person will be asked to remain in jail for a week. Eventually this will create conditions beyond the city's capacity to handle. The strain on the city will be sufficient to force them to negotiate and desegregate. That was the plan; that's what we did; and that's what happened – at least as far as the law was concerned.

Whether it was six or seven to be arrested on the first day, I cannot remember exactly. I know that the group was to have Dr. King, someone else from SCLC, and at least one black man and woman from St. Augustine, a white woman, and a white man. I suspect that the black members of the group from SCLC and St. Augustine had been determined prior to the rally. In any case, that piece was handled efficiently. Then a white woman in her 20s from Ohio quickly volunteered. That left the white man slot. I no longer am certain whether or not I was the only white man present, but I can say that I think I was the only white man there and I know I felt that I was the only white man within blocks of the church. Every eye seemed to be focused on me. It was clear to all, I was the white guy Dr. King had in mind!

I remember sleeping well that night. I was excited, but at peace. I carried no sense of fear or anxiety. This was foolishness; not strength, wisdom, or nobility. For a short time, I lived in the satisfaction of the moment. It comforted me to play a small role in such a significant undertaking; I was not troubled. The next morning, without Dr. King, we met for breakfast and training in non-violence – how to remain centered, how to protect ourselves, why our commitment to the discipline of non-violence was essential. Near lunchtime, Dr. King joined us and we headed off to a well-known, local restaurant.

We were greeted. They attempted to seat us separately by race. Dr. King insisted that we were one party wanting to be seated together. They said that was not possible and we'd have to leave. We then took seats together at one table in the white section of the restaurant. Within minutes the sheriff was there and we were arrested. SCLC, of course, had informed the national media. They were present throughout this brief, dramatic encounter. I was taken away in a car with a black woman from St. Augustine. They shut the car door on her ankle and she was in pain. In Quakertown, Dad was asleep on his recliner chair. Mother watched the news on NBC and was certain it was me she saw being arrested. She cried, probably prayed, and, I believe, said nothing to anyone. Only years later did we discuss this. Even then, I could still feel her pain and suffering.

The emotional pitch was high, but I still felt little fear. I felt more ornery and hopeful. I was much more focused on what was about to be accomplished than on my own circumstances. And it never once crossed my mind that Mother had seen me on the news. All of that quickly changed. Within minutes of our arrival at the St. John's County Jail, I realized something I had never previously considered. Here I was in the segregated south fighting against segregation but it had never occurred to me that prisoners in the jail would be segregated by race. They were. And I now was the frightened white guy!

It turns out, even after fear entered my life, I still had more to fear than I realized. I was an outsider pressing for change among southern white criminals on a dimension of life that, to a man, they took for granted as the way things should be. This created an intense bond between the jailed and the jailers against me, and left me without any reliable protection. There were eleven men in my block; or, as they saw it, ten men and a rat.

We shared a common day room, a toilet, and four cells, each with four bunks. My only reliable protection was that I had a cell to myself and the guards did lock my cell door every night. So, if I curled up in the back corner of my bunk to sleep, no one could reach me through the bars. My cell was the only one locked. Conveniently, the other three were closed but not locked. This made conjugal visits possible. One man provided the sexual release required by the others. I don't know how many others, but it was not a monogamous arrangement.

On two occasions, later the first day and the second day, all of us who had been arrested at the restaurant were brought together for photographs, finger-printing, and legal processing. As I recall, there were three criminal misdemeanor charges brought against us and bail was set at $200 per charge. The National Council of Churches was prepared to provide bail, but the goal was to fill the jail and choke the system. We had pledged to stay for seven days.

During these two periods when we were together, I had my most meaningful and impressionistic contacts with Dr. King. He was calm, warm, confident, and purposeful. It was settling just to be in his presence. There were two specific discussions I vividly remember. The third volume of Paul Tillich's <u>Systematic Theology</u>, on Christian ethics, had just been published. Although I cannot remember specific elements of the discussion, I was impressed with the focus and intensity with which Dr. King engaged Tillich's work. He spoke of an insight he received from Tillich that he wanted to develop in his own thought. Surely this reveals more about me than about Dr. King, but I was astonished at how deeply relevant his theological and philosophical perspectives were to his sense of his work, his purpose and himself.

The other discussion was more strategic. Within several days of our arrest, Dr. King was scheduled to receive an honorary doctoral degree from Yale. Dr. King hoped that Yale's President, Kingman Brewster, would travel to St. Augustine and award the degree to him in jail. This would be a dramatic statement that would capture considerable attention for the campaign and strengthen its momentum. In the end, Brewster decided against such an arrangement and Dr. King left jail early to attend graduation ceremonies in New Haven where he received the honorary degree and spoke about the St. Augustine campaign.

Back in St. John's County, things got quite a bit more difficult. Our cellblock faced the front of the building on the second floor. There was a hallway between our cellblock and the outside wall. The wall consisted of open, louvered windows that permitted me to watch the daily arrival of scores of men and women arrested for violating local segregation laws. The Plan was unfolding as intended. The guards and the other prisoners became increasingly irritable. Even from my isolated perch, I could sense the unsettling shifts that were occurring all around me.

Within my cellblock, I faced challenges and made bad choices. I was universally hated and denied access to soap, toilet paper, toothbrush, and towel. For my part, I was aggressively silent.

Simultaneously, I wanted to say nothing that would further offend them and wanted them to feel in my silence the depth of my disdain for them. There was no pressure to do so, but there had been a suggestion that we consider fasting while in prison. Even without a good reason for doing so, I decided to fast as suggested. Under my circumstances, fasting was a pointless gesture that only further aggravated the other prisoners and damaged by own coping skills.

Hunger soon became the least of my problems. I felt hunger for less than two days – quite manageable. I soon became weak, more in mind than in body. For example, after the third day I could no longer read. I saw and recognized words, but I could not concentrate and maintain attention for more than a sentence or two at a time. I was reading a biography of Gandhi, but seemingly read the same sentences over and over without comprehension. I felt lethargic more than tired; inattentive more than sleepy. I was able to write, but nothing thoughtful or analytical. I could write descriptively about almost everything and anything around me. I retain little of those writings today.

I think it was during the fifth day that hell broke loose. I was sitting at the long metal table at the end of the day room near my cell silently writing. The rest was rapid fire. I don't have memories of sequences, only of experiential blocks. Richard, a tall, skinny, middle-aged man who endlessly paced around me, had me pinned against the sidewall. He had a small knife pressed against my neck beneath my jawbone. I remember his rage – how intensely he hated me. He hated my silence; my endless writing; and his feeling of being judged by me. He screamed that he "hated all 'niggers' regardless of their color."

And then the most improbable of all things actually happened. One of the other prisoners, a 20-year-old from Jessup, Georgia who killed his girlfriend because "she wouldn't fuck," jumped Richard, took the knife from him, and threw it out into the hallway. Neglecting me, he lectured Richard. As corny and lacking in credibility as it is, I still retain a clear sense of what he said. It was something close to the following: "I hate that son-of-a-bitch as much as you. I want him out of here. But I'm sick and tired of you pacing up and down all day. And as much as I hate that fucker, he has as much a right to his opinions as you and I. Leave him alone and stop your shit." It probably was a lot more vulgar, but that is the essence of what he said. If anyone put that into a movie, the audience would boo for being fake and implausible. But in that cell, it gave me the only protection I had. It's strange knowing that my life was directly protected by a murderer who hated me.

A day before my week was completed, another white guy was brought to our cellblock from the protestors. He was from somewhere in New England, about 19 or 20 years old, and seemed to be constitutionally unable to stop talking. Within a very short time, the other prisoners made me feel they now appreciated my silence, but it was too late for us to bond! I was leaving. My release was efficient and uneventful. Someone drove me from the jail to the community center where we had worked on the newspaper and prepared for our arrests. They fed us, but I could barely eat. I drank soda and ate a few bites. I wanted to get away and be by myself. Unfortunately, I had promised the girl from Ohio that I would drive her to Atlanta. I kept my word, dropped her off, and headed north through the Blue Ridge Parkway. There, in a misty forest setting, I found a simple country church with an unlocked door. I peacefully rested there for more than ten hours unable to distinguish my memories, my thoughts, and my dreams.

CHAPTER 4
Boggs Academy, Keysville, Georgia
September,1964 to August, 1965

My arrival at Boggs has not escaped by memory. I spent my 24th birthday in a dingy motel in Augusta, preparing for my next day's arrival at Boggs. On the morning of September 1[st,] I drove south to Waynesboro, county seat of Burke County, one of the eight original counties of Georgia and one of the poorest counties in the United States. I got gas and drove around the courthouse square. Just off the square, I was struck by a strange sight. A shop with large plate-glass windows had the words "Whites Only" painted across them. It was a laundromat. I was shocked by the words but even more perplexed by what I actually saw. On the inside, the only people to be seen were five or six black women. How did this work, I wondered? Turns out it was a perfect example of segregationist logic – those black women were doing white folks' wash. Now that explains everything – and nothing.

Just outside Waynesboro, the route to Boggs became a red-dirt road through piney woods and cotton fields. About 18 miles from town coming over a rise I reached a clearing.

Parts of Boggs were on both sides of the road, but most of it was on the left side. Physically it consisted of about 15 mostly red brick buildings on a pleasant but slightly shabby campus. "Settled in" seemed best to describe it.

Boggs was one of a series of schools set up throughout the Deep South around the turn of the 19th and 20th centuries mostly by Episcopalians and Presbyterians. They were boarding schools created to educate black children in areas of America in which there were no other schooling opportunities available to black people at that time. Boggs was operated by the Board of National Missions of the United Presbyterian USA Church. It had 180 students in grades 9 through 12 during my year of service there. It was the only school for black children in east central Georgia accredited by the state of Georgia in 1964. Although there were a handful of students from more advantaged black families, mostly living in Atlanta, overwhelmingly our students were from families that materially had nothing. Their time at Boggs (education, room, board) was paid for by the Presbyterian Church.

Supposedly, public schools were available for educating black children in east central Georgia. But ten years after segregated public schools had been declared to be

unconstitutional, 100% of those schools remained
segregated and unaccredited. Obviously, permitting local
and state communities to desegregate public schools "with
all deliberate speed" created a pace significantly slower than
climate change. Yet, for example, many well-intentioned
people back home in Pennsylvania felt comfortable
counseling blacks to have patience; after all, it takes time to
make these changes, they'd be told. At this pace, however,
the time it would take to desegregate public schools within
the requirements of the U. S. Constitution can be precisely
calculated – forever and ever! Sounds more like a prayer
than accountable public action. And I suspect that's a pace
few of us would find acceptable if it was our children and
grandchildren and great grandchildren who needed to be
patient and accept the solace of prayer.

I immediately sensed that my presence at Boggs was both
welcomed and a source of anxiety. They needed my
services but were concerned how the community would
respond to me and how effectively I would be able to serve
the school and its students. It turns out that a white man
from New Jersey had worked in my position the previous
year and it had not gone especially well. Few details were
ever discussed with me, but it was clear that he had not
been an effective teacher and had never integrated himself

27

into the life of the school or broader communities. Dr.
Charles Francis, the school's Superintendent, reflected the
attitude of the entire staff – welcome, but….! In my first
meeting with him, he offered to sit in on my classes to
ensure good behavior by the students. I thanked him, told
him that would not be necessary, and suggested that if it
became necessary he should send me back to where I came
from. His response was a nervous laugh. Rev. Ellis, my
supervisor for clergical responsibilities, responded similarly.

My assignments for the first semester included teaching a 9th
grade New Testament class and a senior level English class,
serving as faculty advisor for the student newspaper and
yearbook, conducting daily chapel services, and ministering
to the UPUSA congregation in Waynesboro. I'm proud to
say that I never had a single behavioral difficulty with
students, individually or in groups, in any context –
classroom, campus, dormitory. Dr. Francis and Rev. Ellis
quickly noticed and seemed to be relieved. I had no magic
recipe for the work ahead of me. I simply committed
myself to do the best I could to live and work according to
four guidelines: believe in the potential of my students, be
positive, be fair, and maintain high expectations. I did not
always live up to those standards as well as I aspired to do,

but I always tried to keep them at the center of who I was and what I did. They served me well.

Without a doubt, the hardest part of my time at Boggs was from mid-September through the end of October. Nothing remarkable happened then, but the adjustment was wrenching. I often think of people who celebrate radical individualism. I never felt more like I was just one, all alone. I felt no desire to celebrate. I was not black. I had established no credible place in the black community. I had no place in the white community. I would accept no place in the white community. I felt estranged from the world I left behind. I loved my family but felt they didn't understand me, feeling more rejected by me than loved. I was losing my faith. And to top it all off, I didn't like myself very much. I was *just* an individual and it was hell. It's bad enough to be radically alone; it's even worse to question and dislike the person you're alone with. That was my life.

By November, every one of these realities remained true. Every one retained its sting. Just living day to day didn't wipe them away, but it did soften and reposition them. The slow, almost imperceptible, process of building new realities began to ameliorate the pain of the old realities. I began to learn a bit about my students. Betty Reynolds occasionally made eye contact with me. Sylvester Ginn poured out his hopes for a college education. William Hamilton worried that I, like so many other whites, would betray him. Leon German tried to con me. Eugene Lang wanted to learn about me and be reflective about himself. Other teachers and staff started to laugh at and with me. Meal times became more pleasant even if the food seemed to become more uneatable. I danced with Mrs. Robinson although it required her to take the lead. Dr. Francis cried about the unrealized potential buried in the cemeteries of Burke County. My congregation found me to be inscrutable but they protected me. Late one Friday night a group of black teenage boys in Waynesboro bought me a burger and fries when they learned I was teaching at Boggs. A new world, not so radically individual, was beginning to be built adjacent to the isolation of the old world.

Also, by November, I learned to stay away from Waynesboro as much as possible. Nothing good ever came from my outings there. My first trip to a barbershop convinced me it was time to give up my buzz-cut, flattop. Hateful words and a threatening razor blade did the trick. Fortunately, the guys in the dorm let me use their Tuxedo jell to train my longer hair into a part. Twice I was taken to jail just to harass me. My memory of the first time is quite faded, but I remember the second time vividly. One of my students was in the hospital in Waynesboro. After my last class, I drove into town to see him. When I came out of the hospital there were two officers waiting for me. According to them I was selling without a permit. I said I wasn't selling anything. They looked through my briefcase, finding only class notes and a Bible. Several hours later I was released. The man who spoke said I was selling ideas that people in Waynesboro don't want to buy. My occasional outings away from campus from then on were only to Augusta and Atlanta., except for my Sunday responsibilities at the church in Waynesboro.

The surest evidence of my waning internal suffering was the strengthening of my ability to meet external challenges. Such challenges were omnipresent in ways large and small, subtle and coarse, direct and indirect. A good example was the tradition of "Anniversary Week" celebrations among the local black churches. Each church designated a week to celebrate the anniversary of its founding. Worship services were held every evening of that week and throughout the day on Anniversary Sunday. The host church identified a guest church for each of the evening services. It was expected that members of the guest church's congregation

31

would join the host congregation for the service. The guest church's minister always offered the evening's sermon.

The Presbyterian Church I served in Waynesboro was asked to participate in almost every Anniversary Week celebration. Our membership included the most privileged black residents of the county – a dentist and many teachers. This created an impossible challenge for me. Neither Yale nor my own life experiences had prepared me to preach in a style that related to their traditions and preferences. Trying to find adjustments that would reach out to them without turning myself into a parody or fraud was stressful. It was clear they endured my sermons to get to the offering. The evening of our participation always generated the highest level of giving and had something to do with why we had been invited. This was the most painful part of the evening for me. It was expected I would work the crowd and expand the kitty. You know – "Brothers and sisters, God loves us, we need to do more to show our love for Him. God has been good to us, we need to be good to Him and His servants here at Bethel Baptist church. Brother Jones, I know you have a generous heart. Is it at peace or does it whisper encouragement for you to give even more? Sister Williams, so many of your students come from Bethel families. Helping them tonight is another way for them to grow stronger. Bless you. Bless you." I no longer needed theological doubts or hypocrisy to convince me I was not made to be a minister.

Perhaps my most gifted student was Betty Reynolds. She was the daughter of sharecroppers from southern Burke County. Her inner life was rich and dynamic. None of that was readily apparent from the outside, however. Other than an occasional gesture of disdain, she inserted none of her inherent vitality into the world around her – with one exception. She wrote exceptionally moving poetry and short stories. They all had a few things in common: credibility, torment, and resistance. She, single-handedly, made my work with the students on the newspaper and yearbook rewarding. Slowly, in fits and starts, she permitted a friendship to grow. It was stimulating to listen and to watch her juggle hope and hopelessness. Whenever I doubted Boggs, I remembered Betty.

The issue of attending an integrated college was hard to sort out in 1964. An integrated college meant a historically white college. Historically black colleges were beginning to experience the equivalent of a brain drain. The best and brightest black students were being recruited by schools that, finally, sought integration and decided to expand the availability of educational opportunities. It was hard to differentiate the value of honoring and protecting traditional cultural institutions that had offered committed service to a people, and the importance for each individual to have full access to the best possibilities for growth that will form their lives. I worked with two seniors on their college searches and applications, Betty and Eugene. Betty attended and graduated from Drew University. Eugene attended and graduated from Wesleyan University.

As part of that process, something happened that haunts me to this day and from which I have not released myself. I wrote to William Jones about Betty and Eugene. He was the Director of Admissions at Ursinus College, my alma mater. He didn't respond. He didn't even send the application forms I had requested. I believe I wrote to him three times. Eventually I got a hand-written note saying he did not think these students were admissible and that applying would be a waste of their time and money. Ursinus had been good to me and for me. It gave me a bridge that contributed immeasurably to my growth and to important transitions in my life. Even though I suspect that Ursinus was and is better than William Jones and I carry a clear and strong sense of appreciation for what it made possible for me, I find it exceedingly difficult to reconnect with it or to offer any gesture of support for it. Forty-five years later, I fear it may be sheer stubbornness that keeps me estranged, but I remind myself that stubbornness will always be one of my limitations but it will never be my worst failure.*

Note: thanks to the healing grace of a mentor of mine at Ursinus, Richard Schellhase, I have reconnected with Ursinus and now support funding for diversity scholarships there.

On a cold, dreary Saturday in mid-January, walking across the Boggs campus I ran into the niece of Dr. Martin Luther King, Jr. Dr. King's brother and father lived in Atlanta and had arranged for her education at Boggs. In fact, later that spring I was able to meet her parents and Dr. King Sr. in Atlanta. She was a 9th grader in my religion class. We exchanged pleasantries and then her expression became intensely serious. I distinctly remember her words. She said, "Mr. Hoffert you go to Yale. Do you think we are inferior?" How do you begin to answer such a question in a way that not only speaks the truth you believe but in a way that puts her doubts to rest and she can trust? How does such a question get formulated in a girl from a strong and loving family? Who takes responsibility for creating a world that would make such a question so painful, so haunting, and so possible to her? I don't know what all I said, but we talked for hours.

I was able to add another teaching responsibility for the spring semester. Dr. Francis wanted Boggs to offer a "Negro History" course. No one on the staff was properly prepared to teach such a course. To Dr. Francis this was unfortunate, but it should not be an impediment for doing what needed to be done. His greater disappointment was that I was the only one willing to teach such a course. It was a testimony to his commitment to the project that he agreed to let me try. I cannot overstate my complete incompetence in the subject matter. I offered nothing more than a willingness to take it on and an eagerness to learn. Fortunately, my students assumed nothing of me other than that I'd provide the opportunity for all of us to learn together something we felt intensely compelled to know. I learned a lesson that applies equally to teachers and to students: there is no more exciting educational experience than one in which teaching and learning are vitally and simultaneously connected.

On a cold night near the end of February 1965 around 10:30, I was in the Boggs chapel office sitting at the typewriter pecking out notes for my morning chapel talk.

The space heater was on "Hi" and the blinds closed tight.
It was a bit later than usual, but otherwise a night like
almost all others. Little did I know that in a moment it
would be a night unlike any other. Suddenly there was a
loud explosion and a flash of light that seemed to penetrate
the blinds. I lifted them and saw about five men (I never
was sure exactly how many there were) running past the
gym through pine trees to trucks parked on the lane just
west of Rev. Ellis' home. Bright orange flames silhouetted
the gym.

As the trucks sped away, I ran outside. I was the first one at
the school coming from my direction. Others arrived in the
opposite direction from the dormitories. The entire school
building was engulfed with flames. There were fire hydrants
but no fire trucks or firefighters. The closest fire company,
in Waynesboro, refused to come out to Boggs. We were
paralyzed with an overwhelming sense of helplessness. We
did wrap a chain around a walkway roof that connected the
school with the gym, using a tractor to pull away the roof.
That probably saved the gym, but everything else was a total
loss. In less than an hour it was over except for embers that
smoked for days.

Even when there are warning signs of danger, something like this still hits you as a shocking surprise. Tacit violence and hostility was a constant companion of everyday life. We were well aware that these charged situations often transform themselves into explicit attacks. Several days earlier, it turns out, we had been given our specific warning. We were shaken but hadn't realized the full implications of a cross burning by the local KKK immediately outside the boys' dormitory where I lived. The Klan's ceremonial cross burning felt like such a violation in itself. We hadn't considered it as merely a prologue. In any case, it's hard to imagine the hatred and twisted understandings that drive anyone to do such things under the sign of the cross.

I believe the fire was on a Wednesday evening. In any case, we held regular classes on the following Monday. We used the dormitories, the dining hall, the gym, the chapel, and the student center. Schedules had to be adjusted, but we made it work. Everyone pitched in; everyone did their part to make it work. There were no complaints; just steadfast determination to prevail and move ahead. For example, most of the work on the yearbook had been completed and was ready to be sent to the publisher/printer. Now everything was lost. Immediately, Betty rallied us to put together an alternate, soft-covered yearbook. We did it and it's one of my cherished possessions.

It's hard to measure the loss. One reflection of it is to consider the school's library. In the previous 49 years of the school's existence, it had never been able to purchase new books for the library. All of its books had been donations, mostly from Christian missionary societies in northern Presbyterian churches. In 1964-65, Boggs had its first budget to buy new books for the library. We worked diligently to get as many books as possible that would serve our greatest educational needs. Ironically, a major shipment of new books arrived just before the fire and were destroyed. Within days after the fire, we set about rebuilding the library the way our library had been built in the past – from donations. The response was so strong, Dr. Francis sent me up to the New Jersey/Pennsylvania area with the school's flatbed truck to bring back a load of books. He sent a student, Thomas Duvall, with me. Thomas was very fair skinned. We spent a night at my home in Quakertown. In the morning, Mother whispered to me, "Bob I thought you said all the students at your school were Negroes?" "Mother, they are. As Dr. Francis says, their color varies so much because they are all *American* Negroes." Upon our return, I spent almost every spare moment of my remaining time at Boggs beneath the gym bleachers sorting and cataloguing books to reestablish a working library at Boggs.

In April of 1965, Dr. Francis asked me to drive the music teacher, Ms. Gadsden, and two of her piano students to Savannah for a performance competition. Savannah was about 100 miles south of Boggs. We left early on a Saturday morning and returned late the same day. The excitement, we assumed, would be from the competition. Both students were quite talented. We had every reason to expect them to compete well. They did, but the source of excitement was unexpected. On our way to Savannah, we became aware of a car tailing closely behind us. That went on for miles. Occasionally he moved out to pass us but instead of passing tried to push us off the highway. Finally, he did pass us and sped ahead. About five minutes later we came upon him standing on the side of the road waving a gun. I had Ms. Gadsden and the girls hit the floor. We sped past. I don't believe he fired the gun. We never saw him again, but we never were quite the same.

Following the school's graduation ceremony, I had a major period of depression. I had to remain at Boggs for the summer program. Everyone else returned to their homes for the summer for a two-week break before returning to Boggs. I was physically and psychically alone. Beyond anything I had imagined, I had bonded with my students and co-workers. My new sense of loss and loneliness sickened me. Fortunately, two weeks actually is not a long time even when, in the midst of it, it feels interminable. Soon some students returned and I was in charge of recreational activities for them while they completed their study and work responsibilities. I had access to a VW bus. We'd pile in and head out for fun.

Trouble was, it wasn't always fun that we found. Take swimming for example. We had to drive 50 miles to the closest public swimming pool available for blacks. No one complained or even commented about that. But those 50 miles created many opportunities for others to take the fun out of our trip. It was mostly young white boys. They'd try to drive us off the road, they'd scream obscenities, they displayed their middle fingers, and, most manly of all, they'd moon us. It quickly got old and wearisome. And that doesn't even touch the depth of disrespect for my students' humanity that was expressed and impressed.

One day we were playing softball. The catcher was a spunky kid who played aggressively and was up to any competitive challenge. An older boy was at bat. He swung and connected well. In his excitement, he let his bat fly, hitting the catcher's eye. Blood spurted everywhere. The kids rallied to help and immediately got me a compress. As soon as things had settled a bit, the injured boy and I headed off to see the doctor in Waynesboro. It was a bad cut but the boy was calm. When we arrived at the doctor's office I was confronted by a difficulty I had not anticipated. There were two waiting rooms – "White" and "Colored". I was white and he was colored but what really mattered was that we needed to be together and he needed care. I decided to go into the Colored waiting room. That was the wrong choice according to the nurse. Our exchange was unpleasant and I lied. She swallowed my lie and things got even worse. Eventually we did get to what really mattered – taking care of the boy.

Overall, my summer at Boggs was supposed to be a quiet time. There would be plenty of opportunities to read and relax while the students worked during the days. But that is not the summer that actually materialized. President Johnson's Great Society programs were coming to life. One of the best known of those programs was Head Start. If there was anywhere in the country that could benefit from Head Start, it certainly was Burke County, Georgia. Local

Head Start programs could be organized by public or private agencies. In Burke County, black leaders initiated a program much to the dismay and opposition of established city and county leaders (white) who had complete satisfaction with things as they were. This Old Guard knew how to play dirty pool. They simultaneously organized a boycott of the program by local whites and tried to close down the program with the feds claiming it was not integrated! No matter how hard the program organizers tried, they were unable to attract either white students or white teachers. Dr. Francis came to me. Would I be willing to teach in the Head Start program, he asked? Yes, I said. I was the integration they needed to keep going.

Once again, I found myself teaching in a context for which I was totally unprepared. It's hard to exaggerate the impressionability of those children. To be able to offer them positive, unfamiliar impressions had remarkable and immediate effects on them. There was no question that the program had transforming potential for their lives. There was only a question how long these changes could be sustained outside the support and reinforcement of the program.

We had home visits for each of our children. They were difficult for me and for the parents. I wanted to be involved, but not intrusive. Parents knew the limitations of their circumstances, but were proud. Two home visits stand out with special intensity for me. While visiting the one room home of a boy in my class, a huckster came by in his truck. The mother bought five watermelons for a dollar. The situation was uncomfortable for her. Turning to me she said, "I know it's not the best but it's all I have and it fills their tummies." Angela Fair was a precious, wispy child. Her mother cried tears of joy that Angela was in Head Start and shared her hopes for Angela's future. Almost, she said, Angela wasn't able to be in the program. She had only one dress. It wasn't until a neighbor handed down a second dress that it was possible for her to attend, alternating wearing and cleaning days for the two dresses.

I left Boggs fatigued, anxious, and changed. Driving back on that red-dirt road to Waynesboro on my way to I-95 north, it never occurred to me that there might be one last surprise waiting for me. I wanted nothing more than to fill my VW beetle's gas tank and get on the road for home. Instead, I was delayed a bit. In clock time, only a few minutes. In reflection time, I can't calculate how long. Two men in a four-door sedan pulled up next to me. The driver got out of the car. He wore a dark blue suit and came up directly to me. He told me his name, showed me a badge, and said he worked for the FBI. For more than a month, he claimed, I had been followed. He didn't explain why, but said he was pleased I was leaving town. I didn't feel similarly.

Robert W. Hoffert

CHAPTER 5
New Haven and Cincinnati,
September 1965 to August 1966

My return north and to Yale was torturous. I felt out of
place and feared that anything I did would betray the people
at Boggs and my experiences with them. I feared
friendships and personal relationships that might associate
me with actions and beliefs that would violate my
commitments. My room in Taylor House at Yale was the
first room at the top of the stairs. The room at the bottom
of the stairs had the following information posted on the
door, "Benjamin T. Jordan Jr. Macon, Georgia. Southern
Baptist." I thought I was going to lose my mind. Right
beneath me lived the personification of everything that had
caused so much pain for me and everyone else I cared about
at Boggs.

I would have nothing to do with him. Others in the house
were concerned thinking that my response to Ben was
uncharacteristic of me and unfair to him. He was a decent
and interesting guy they insisted. Bull shit, I insisted. My
only memory is that one Friday evening just before a

holiday break I was returning to my room from dinner. Ben
and I accidentally met in the hallway and had an initial,
awkward interchange on the stairs. For reasons beyond
comprehension, both of us struggled to communicate.
Hours later we knew we had launched an important
relationship. Ben became and remains a dear friend. In
fact, he was the only Christian I knew who I'd permit to
marry me. On May 15, 1971, the Reverend Benjamin T.
Jordan Jr. of Macon, Georgia, now United Church of
Christ, married Maureen and Bob in State College,
Pennsylvania.

My return to Yale for my last year of studies often felt like a
masochistic exercise. Prudence brought me back to
complete my degree, I claimed. But was it prudent to finish
a program of study that had become utterly unsuited for
who I was becoming and wanted to be? I had no idea at
that time how valuable my theological education would be
to my subsequent studies in political philosophy.

Eventually, with help from a remarkable man at Yale,
Professor William Muehl, I finally committed myself to a
course of action designed to resolve my struggles with my
parents, especially my Dad. I terminated my "care"
relationship with the Philadelphia Presbytery, and accepted

a summer position as a minister at a Presbyterian church in St. Bernard (Cincinnati), Ohio. I was hired by the Board of National Missions, UPUSA. My job was to close down the church. I could do that! My hope was that this gesture would satisfy my Dad's continuing need for me to serve as a minister.

The Board of National Missions had contacted me about this job in St. Bernard based on their familiarity with my work for them at Boggs Academy. However, there was a twist to this position. In St. Bernard, I would be working with a completely white congregation that was outspokenly racist. For example, prior to my arrival in June, a visiting minister who was conducting a Sunday morning service had several congregants loudly stamp their feet and others walk out when, in the course of his prayer, he asked for God's guidance and blessings on the newly elected Moderator of the General Assembly – a black man. The congregation was no longer able to sustain itself financially and was operated by the Board. My job was to bring it to a successful closure. Overall, the whole situation was a maze of paradoxes. Most paradoxical of all, working to shut down a church satisfied my parents' need for me to serve as the minister of a church!

Even working with a group of people from whom I was alienated in many significant ways, created unexpected bonds. Two examples remain with me. One Sunday, I preached a sermon using a text from Karl Marx. It was from the last paragraph of his Third Manuscript essay on "Money." It expresses a moving tribute to the authenticity of true love. I did not identify the passage's source. Knowing that the congregation assumed it was biblical, perhaps even from a letter of Paul, gave me cynical satisfaction in the short run, but, over time, has disturbed me for not honoring them and for being inauthentic while preaching to them in behalf of authenticity.

The other example relates to Gus Backer. Gus was a member of the church's congregation. He was in failing health and I visited him regularly. When he died, the family asked me to conduct his funeral service. I was horrified. I told them that I could not do that because I was not ordained. They called the Board and were told there was no reason why I could not conduct the service. I can still feel the agony of trying to be true to myself and trying to serve a grieving family. My regret is that I may have failed on both counts.

I accomplished the job I was sent to do in St. Bernard. St. Bernard UPUSA was closed. Mother and Dad visited me, went to a service I conducted, and took pictures of the church bulletin board that said: "Robert Hoffert, minister." The burden of my being a minister relaxed. In fact, it never again had its prior intensity with my parents. But I was living episodes; not building a life. Now what? It was my good fortune that another episode unexpectedly presented itself to me.

The Woodrow Wilson Fellowship Foundation had a program designed to encourage African Americans who had recently completed a graduate degree to return to traditionally black colleges and universities to teach. Their purpose was two-fold: to provide model teachers and to encourage and prepare black students for graduate and professional studies. The Woodrow Wilson people had been trying to place someone in one of the historically black state schools in Alabama, but without success. Now they had an opportunity to do so, but had no African American graduate to fill it. A friend of mine from Yale was aware of these circumstances and knew they were willing to appoint a white person just to get someone affiliated with their program in the door. Several phone calls later it was set. On September 1, 1966, I would begin service at Alabama

A & M in Huntsville (Normal, actually) as an assistant professor of philosophy and a Woodrow Wilson Foundation Fellow.

CHAPTER 6
Alabama A & M University, Huntsville, Alabama
1966 to 1968

Having broken the ice earlier by writing about my experiences in St. Augustine and at Boggs Academy, I am now a bit more comfortable trying to share my more unfocused and complex experiences at Alabama A & M University from September, 1966 thru September, 1968. In Alabama, my experiences at the University and living in George Wallace country were more directly intertwined with my faith struggles, with the form and direction of my personal life, and with my search for the understanding of my parents. Boggs diverted my attention from these personal matters, but it did not resolve the stresses and doubts they raised in my life.

My arrival at A & M reflects the new challenges I would face but had not anticipated. I drove onto campus without directions or a specific destination, knowing only that I had to arrive by the afternoon of the 1st and that the school would provide housing for me. The campus, north of Huntsville, sits on the side of a hill overlooking the city. I pulled into a parking spot next to the student center. A light-skinned black man wearing a white suit with a wide brimmed white hat appeared and said simply, "welcome to the place." He introduced himself as Richard Morrison, the president of the university.

There were five white professors at A & M during the two years I was there. One preceded the rest of us (in history), two others arrived with me (in physics and sociology), another one came in the spring semester of my first year (in political science), and, of course, myself. My position – not so much me – was a source of controversy. My tie to the Woodrow Wilson Foundation was the primary issue. Campus and State administrators had resisted affiliations, of any sort. They saw the Woodrow Wilson program as an "outsiders'" agenda that would fuel discontent, foster pressures for change, and generally make the status quo more insecure. Reluctantly, they turned to me at the last minute because of their inability to find anyone prepared to teach a new, state-mandated course in philosophy and logic that now was required of every first-year student enrolled at all state colleges and universities in Alabama starting Fall, 1966.

School officials had no idea just how thin my own credentials were for the responsibilities of this appointment. But this job gave me a great opportunity to learn basic syllogistic logic and deductive reasoning, as well as an overview of the primary sub-fields of philosophy. The leadership culture at A & M was uncomfortable both with what I taught and my non-instructional links and purposes. I always felt that everything about me, for them, was unsettling. Although, as an individual, I was always treated appropriately.

My reflections about Alabama A & M are not organized historically or chronologically; that is, they do not follow a somewhat linear timeline. They are a collage of memories – not random, but thematic more than sequential. They tend to be organized in two broad clusters: "people" and "special circumstances/events."

People

Dr. Tambi, a new faculty member in education from India via North Carolina; Jerry Shipman, a new faculty member in mathematics and an undergraduate of Alabama A & M; and myself were assigned to an apartment in faculty housing. Dr. Tambi was an older man, but carried the energy, idealism, and commitment of youth. He had a calming effect on Jerry and I even though "calm" would be an inappropriate description of his own persona.

We had a uniquely stimulating year living together. Unfortunately, our unit of faculty housing had to be released for a family. Jerry and I, with Charles Chabot, rented a house in a black sub-division about a mile south of campus, from an African American army officer. Many of our campus friends enjoyed the opportunity to have a convenient off-campus place for relaxed socializing. Neighbors had mild concerns that whites and blacks living together might stir up outsiders who would disrupt everyday life in their community. Fortunately, none of that ever developed and soon everyone relaxed into a pleasant sociability.

Two students were especially significant for me at A & M – Lonnie Smith and Joe Jennings. Lonnie has remained a dear friend but our friendship never came easily or conventionally. He is blessed with great intelligence, cunning, and decency, but cursed by the trauma of raw poverty and racism, and the completely inadequate development of his core academic skills. He responds to his limitations alternatively with determination as challenges to tackle and defeat, with anger and hostility to their sources, and with self-doubt and self-loathing when he feared they actually might be the truth about himself.

Lonnie sought me out, initially, just to explore his inherent curiosity. Over time, we created a measure of trust – we weren't just a black man and a white man jiving each other. As the trust grew, we became friends. We have remained friends in spite of numerous opportunities to go our separate ways or turn our backs on each other. Here are a few examples of our roller coaster ride. In his junior year, Lonnie became (in his own eyes, at least) a Black Panther. He was energized by this association. His quandary was what did this mean for his friendship with me. At times, he was convinced that he could not continue a friendship with "honky Bob." Eventually, he decided that our friendship could continue.

By the 1970s he turned to religion as a foundation for his life. I have never been able to inspire him to abandon religion! I did try. Respectfully, I hope. My failure in that regard has never damaged our relationship. Some of his religious choices, however, have been stressful for me. In the mid-1970s he became a Mormon. I thought I would lose it. True, I do not admire Mormonism. But I do insist that Mormons must receive the full affirmation and protection that religious liberty in American society provides for all religious beliefs – theirs and mine. My distress about Lonnie's decision was that it was a choice filled with self-contempt. How does one build an authentic life within a tradition in which who you are is excluded from the fullness of membership? At that time, African Americans could not hold the priesthood or participate in most temple ordinances within Mormonism. Further, these racial restrictions only applied to persons of black African descent. I was bewildered and distressed. Soon he became a Roman Catholic – the religion of his new sweetheart and soon to be bride. Throughout the course of the last several decades, it appears, he has settled into some version of his Pentecostal roots. Our friendship has also settled into calm acceptance.

By all accounts, Joe Jennings was the premier player on the A & M football team when I arrived. He was the only player drafted for professional play from the 1966 team – drafted by the Canadian Football League, not the NFL, where he successfully played as a linebacker. Joe took my philosophy class as an elective. When he appeared at my office one day, I knew nothing about him other than that he had written some well-constructed and thoughtful short essays on a recent quiz. Shy and somewhat apologetic, he quietly told me that he would not read the next assignment for my course. If that meant he could not successfully complete the course, he needed to know so he could withdraw. The assignment in question was readings from the letters of Paul in the New Testament of the Christian Bible. He said he thought the Bible was one of the reasons his people were subordinated and wanted nothing to do with it. He would not read it.

It was a long conversation, but eventually I convinced him that his reasons for not reading the Bible were, perhaps, the best reasons for him to read it. If it really was the cause of ills he wanted to contest, was it not in his best interest to know it well to better do battle against it? That's how our friendship began. After that, we talked often. Initially our conversations centered on Christianity, but they expanded into his interest in the arts, especially modern painting, and his frustrations coaching football – "how do you teach a guy things I was born knowing."

Joe was a ruggedly handsome young man, but he had a mouth full of rotten teeth. It became clear that his teeth were contributing to a serious deterioration of his overall health. He had nothing and I had next to nothing to pay for the medical care he required. I visited with a local dentist I knew through the Unitarians. Still, I was unable to find a way to deal with his condition. This led me to meet with a county social worker. I made a pitch built around his health. Much to my shock, she told me there was no program that would help him based on health and economic need. However, there was a program that would cover the costs for his dental care based on cosmetics and economic need. If there was a negative cosmetic impact in his probable work setting and economic need, his dental treatments could be covered. I made the case based on his being a future teacher and all of his dental work was covered. It was easy. I just hadn't thought to look at the cosmetics counter for a solution.

One mid-afternoon I was in my office grading papers. I heard some animated discussion outside my door and recognized three students from my class. Their chatter continued until, finally, they knocked on the door. One of the students, Nat, asked if I could settle their disagreement. I said, "I'll try." He asked, "Is your father the president of a college or the head of a corporation?" "Neither" was my immediate, smiling answer. Then I asked them to explain where those particular options came from. They didn't know. They only knew that both versions were circulating among the students and they wanted to know which one was right. And then Alice added that they knew I had come from something like that because I drove a VW bug and wore the same ratty jacket every day with holes in the elbows – only advantaged white guys would do that. I don't think they ever fully believed that my father was a maintenance man in a paper-processing factory, my mother pressed blouses in a garment factory, and neither of them was educated beyond elementary school.

There were many more students, faculty and staff who created a warm and stimulating world for me – Jerry Shipman, Alice Ward, Claude Holloway, Nat Turner, John Williams, Althea and Lonnie Waites. There were a few for whom I had no respect. Best to leave them nameless.

Special Circumstances/Events

Atlanta was my preferred retreat (nearly 200 miles from A & M), as it was for many students, faculty, and staff. I routinely offered rides for weekend visits. No one ever accepted my invitations, but the reason was not personal.

Huntsville, Atlanta, and Birmingham form a triangle. I always took the shortest route, which was the hypotenuse of the triangle – Huntsville to Atlanta. All of the students, faculty, and staff took the right angle of the triangle – Huntsville to Birmingham to Atlanta – that was almost 50 miles longer. Why? Because my route went through northeast Alabama and northwest Georgia, a region of white, mountain culture in which there were no clear rules of accommodation between whites and blacks. And even in the late 1960s, memories of the Scottsboro boys' fate in 1931 were vivid in Alabama's black communities. Taking the longer route was safer. They knew where they could get gas, use a rest room, or find a bite to eat without incident. Patterns were set, rules were clear, expectations were known. All one had to do was "stay in your place." On the shorter route, they had no place and little to guide safe behavior. The dangers far outweighed the miles saved.

Everyday life while I was at A & M was rather uneventful, routine and even somewhat dull at times. My previous experiences in the south were premised on the pursuit of positive change; at A & M life was premised on keeping things much as they had been and convincing "the Man" that everything was to his satisfaction. In terms of immediate threats and dangers, life was rather safe and somewhat comfortable. In terms of dignity, integrity, pride, and hope, the plug had been pulled and those qualities had been drained from our world. I often felt that we were animated shells for whom the most fundamental truth was simply that we had been emptied.

It's hard to capture a clear sense of what I mean by this. Two examples come to mind that may be helpful. Rocket and space research led by Wernher von Braun at the Redstone Arsenal had created a boomtown atmosphere in Huntsville. As Huntsville and northern Alabama grew, the State saw the need to expand its capacity for higher education in the region. Although the State already had a higher education institution in Huntsville, Alabama A & M University, it talked and acted as if there were none and created the University of Alabama, Huntsville. UAH became the white school and A & M continued to be an almost exclusively black school. UAH received ample state funding; A & M was funded on a starvation diet. It's not surprising that white Alabama leadership in the late 1960s wanted this; it was less understandable, at least to me as a white outsider, that the leadership of A & M was so vigorous in defending the blatant creation of implicit segregation in a supposedly post-segregation era.

Governor George C. Wallace and the state legislature, in another example of the emptied life at A & M, decided that all State schools were required to play the blackface minstrel song "Dixie" before all public meetings, including sporting events. I remember how offended I was and how accepting many of my students and colleagues seemed to be. I don't mean to imply by "accepting" that they liked it or appreciated it, but that it was to be expected and accommodated. I hated it and thought it had to be disrespected in every effective way possible. At the opening football game of the 1966 season, spectators stood and players held their helmets patiently as "Dixie" was played by the A & M marching band to a hushed stadium. At best, it was surreal. More to the point, it was a tolerated violation. I thought I had to scream, but I didn't.

Teaching at Boggs felt like contributing to a process of unlocking the rich potential of our students. Teaching at A & M, in too many cases, felt like contributing to a scandal at the ultimate detriment of our students. Most of my students had been cheated of proper preparation for a college education. Rather than acknowledge that circumstance and redress it so their college education could contribute to a more fulfilling enhancement of their lives, we offered a college education in name. It presented me with a quandary. I was deeply committed to providing opportunities for my students to have a college education and had every reason to trust their potential, but it had to be a college education in substance not just in its outer form or they were being cheated and misled.

At the same time, I had some truly exceptional students. I have never taught at any college-level institution where there was not a distinct polarity between the strongest and the weakest students we were called upon to serve, but nowhere was the polarity as extreme as at A & M. I often think of Nathaniel, Robert, Alice, Claude, and Joe with such fondness and deep respect. They were gifted, well prepared, and hardworking students. They prevailed at exceptionally high levels in spite of what we offered them more than because of what we offered them.

In the late fall of 1967 I got a strange and unexpected phone call. It was from a woman in Florence, Alabama (about 75 miles west of Huntsville). She said that a community group wanted to have a debate about the War in Vietnam. Their problem was that they couldn't find anyone to take the position of opposition to the war. Somehow, she was given my name as someone who might take on that role. The truth is that I was not opposed to the war at that time. In fact, I knew next to nothing about it. My world was small and focused. I was totally absorbed in my teaching and the ways in which it might contribute to enriched opportunities for my students and for a greater measure of social justice in America. Although it embarrasses me now, my implicit view was that attention to the war would divert me from my work and my commitments.

We talked. She said that I didn't have to mean it. They just needed someone to represent that position. Finally, I said that I would not do it. She gave me her phone number and asked me to reconsider. The next day I called her back and agreed to do it. I decided that this was a unique opportunity for me to learn about something I knew nothing about. My age had kept me out of the draft. My work had diverted my attention. And my cause was highly focused. I read voraciously. By the time of the debate, I was not a straw man. I was deeply opposed to the war as it had been "justified" and was being pursued. As Martin Luther King, Jr. said in his 1967 speech "Beyond Vietnam," the war was an instrument of injustice at home against our own people and abroad against other people.

My desire to teach at the college level solidified during my two years at Alabama A & M. That meant I needed to pursue Ph.D. studies. Because my interests centered on political philosophy, I eventually decided to locate my degree program in Political Science – even though I had never pursued studies in that discipline. It turns out, that was the least of my obstacles. In April 1968, Martin Luther King, Jr. was assassinated. In June 1968, Robert F. Kennedy was assassinated. I already lived under the shadow of John F. Kennedy's assassination. It's a challenge to keep alive commitments to public purposes and responsibilities when the clearest and most effective voices of public advocacy are mowed down either by sinister design, intransigent hatred, or random craziness. What happened to me all too closely reflects what happened to America – I went private. I didn't change my commitments, but I gave them more of a personal space than a communal presence. I left Alabama A & M vowing to do my studies diligently, but, as much as possible, I would associate with no one. I swallowed the Kool-Aid that only I could treasure and protect my deepest purposes. It was me – alone. That's the great deception: there is no justice, there is no human dignity, there is no growth in isolation. It's what we achieve together, in public, bumping into each other. That's how we make a difference.

Robert W. Hoffert

CHAPTER 7
Reflections
2009 to 2019

My Uncle Paul's request was two-fold—to share my experiences and to offer a few reflections on them. My reflections cascade and intersect in rich and confusing patterns. Rather than try to sort them out into a contrived organization or capture them all, I will try to limit myself to a few that feel especially salient for me at this particular juncture in my life after decades of digesting.

I wrote the above sections related to my Southern experiences between January 19, 2009 and February 1, 2009 (Florida and Georgia) and between January 8, 2014 and January 11, 2014 (Alabama). Similarly, a substantial part of what follows are reflections written during these two time frames. However, I have been unable to prepare these writings for publication during the 2017 – 2019 timeframe without adding some commentary related to the troubling times we are currently enduring.

I desperately hope I will not be preachy. Opinionated, yes. I'm comfortable being opinionated. Unfortunately, self-satisfaction, self-righteousness, and presumption live in me as they do in others. And they are as distasteful to me in myself as they are to me in others. I live most comfortably with these reflections as conversations with myself. I invite you to listen in and see if and how they make any sense to you.

Racism and Prejudice

America is disfigured by endemic racism and the overt and covert prejudicial attitudes and behaviors that shape and energize it. Perhaps it's just semantics, but I have never been similarly willing to characterize individual American citizens as racists. Neither have I been willing to label them as non-racist. As individual citizens, both orientations have ample presence in our personal lives. We occupy a racist society, but if our inherent personal identity is categorically racist, the battle against racism has been lost and we have denied ourselves credible affirmations and purposes that give us the leverage necessary to battle, reduce, and overcome both the racism that is within us and that has captured our national life. Similarly, if our personal identity is categorically non-racist, we are foolish and blind, and we have refused to see or contest the most detrimental components of our personal lives and our lives as Americans.

To some extent, our personal lives are microcosms of our national life. As I tell my children, please don't remember me just at my best or just at my worst. Both exist. Both are real. Remember me most as the person whose life was a struggle between both of those tendencies and behaviors. Remember those things about me, and reflect on how I handled the struggle between my weaknesses and failures and my strengths and accomplishments in the course of living everyday life. Correspondingly, our national life has been a struggle between both racist and non-racist possibilities. If we remember that tension, we will best position ourselves to strengthen our most honorable heritage and to check the damaging effects of our most shameful traditions, attitudes and habits.

Without a doubt, racism is fueled by hatred and moral degeneracy. These are the characteristics we commonly identify when we accuse others of racism and deny when we exempt ourselves from it. But this creates an incomplete understanding of the problem of racism. The problem of racism is inherent in the processes of human knowledge and understanding. Even before I explain what I mean by that claim, let me insist that this does not excuse racism or exempt it from contempt. The fact that we do not possess the perfection of the gods, does not lessen or eliminate our moral responsibility. In fact, our lack of perfection is why our moral accountability is necessary – we don't automatically know or do the right or best thing; we make choices for which we must be answerable.

Whether racism and prejudice are manifested formally or informally, structurally or functionally, we normally approach racism and prejudice as problems of values. And, surely, they are value problems. All structures of racism and prejudice have normative elements embedded at their core according to which categories of superior and inferior, pure and impure, and chosen and rejected are asserted. Yet, contesting racism and prejudice on a values battlefield seems futile.

Look at our own society, for example. More than three out of four Americans claim some form of association with Christianity. The values taught by the New Testament are unambiguous – God loves us all equally and we are all

God's children it claims. The Christian Bible teaches a universal message of God's inclusive love. But Christianity as practiced by Christians frequently offers a dark reflection of those teachings and often presents itself as an aggressive denial of them that is shocking to many non-Christians and atheists. Consequently, I believe it is necessary to explore an expanded context for examining and understanding racism and prejudice – one largely informed by Gordon Allport's study of prejudice.

> *Allport, Gordon W.* **The Nature of Prejudice**, *Addison-Wesley, 1954.*

Functional knowledge is impossible for human beings without the use of generalizations. Any alternative is functionally impossible; that is, we will never know every specific instance of any sizable category. For example, I am a 79-year-old Caucasian male of German heritage and American citizenship. Neither you nor I know every other person who shares those characteristics with me. We don't even know how many of us there are. Yet, both you and I, create generalizations about my sub-category as well as about men and women, Christians and Muslims, whites and blacks, natives and immigrants, Republicans and Democrats, hippies and rednecks, Millennials and Baby Boomers, and conservatives and liberals.

In every one of these cases, there are three things that are true.

1. None of us know all of the specific members of the generalized group.

2. Not all specific members of any generalized group are the same.

3. Although imprecise, generalizations are essential tools for functional knowledge of each other and our world.

At one level, profiling is an inherent component of human knowing.

The irony is that a process essential for practical human life can also be so damaging and destructive of human life. Generalizations make it possible for us to know the world and through that knowledge to function in the world effectively. What happens relative to racism and prejudice is that fear, a lack of familiarity, fixed attitudes, ignorance, and a paucity of curiosity about the unknown combine to create generalizations that become rigid and impervious to evidence. This is the genesis and essence of racism and prejudice.

American Christians know that there are all kinds of Christians, but commonly insist on seeing Muslims as a much more homogenized group. Heterosexuals know their category includes everything from the abstinent to the promiscuous, but often find it easy to see homosexuals as uniformly promiscuous. Privileged citizens savoring their gourmet meals find it easy to project shiftless irresponsibility onto the immigrant workers who toiled to provide the food they enjoy in sumptuous leisure. In all these cases and countless others, we acknowledge the specific variabilities of our own group and project a false, usually negative, uniformity on the targeted groups.

Racism and prejudice are not only results of the ironic consequences of generalizations; they are also the results of a refusal to accept responsibility for unintended consequences. We claim to intend no harm. There usually are some threads of evidence for most racist and prejudicial generalizations. But then we stop and give them little or no attention.

We don't want to take the next step. We intend no harm, but harm is done. And we pursue no corrective. We can site the evidence that supports our prejudice, but have no curiosity about contrary evidence, the sufficiency of our evidence, or the factors that generated the evidence we site. In short, we refuse to accept responsibility for the unintended consequences of our choices, and are comforted by self-righteousness because of the presumed purity and nobility of the intentions we attribute to ourselves.

At this point we can see that racism and prejudice are not only grounded in how we know the world and see each other, but also in how we know ourselves. We know ourselves on the most favorable of terms. We know ourselves within a richness of specifics unlike our knowledge of any other. We know ourselves with a sense of completeness and with little or no sense of missing anything of significance.

Nevertheless, how we know ourselves shapes how we know others. Simply put, the more penetrating, circumspect and questioning we are within the knowing of ourselves, the more expansive are the possibilities for knowing the fullness of others. The more superficial, unreflective, and rigid we are within the knowing of ourselves, the less expansive are the possibilities for knowing others.

When I claimed that the foundation of racism and prejudice is in structures of human knowing, I was pointing to the necessity of generalizations and the uniqueness of self-knowledge. Both are essential and inevitable. And both have the potential for destructive distortions. In many respects, the first question is not whether I want to do the right or good thing, but do I want to know the world and myself, not just within the comfort zone of my current knowledge, but also within a zone of enhanced precision and reliability. If we can't shed the comfort of the familiar for the sake of more precise and granulated understandings, there is little hope for lessening the twisted impacts of racism and prejudice even as we sit in largely segregated churches singing hymns praising God's love for all his children.

Prior to an engagement of our values, we need to consider how we are positioned in terms of knowledge:

- Is my knowing defined more by fear of the unknown or by curiosity to know more better?
- Do I have an active interest in testing my knowledge and expanding the limits of my knowledge?
- Am I willing to consider the variability of specific cases that I know to be true about my own groups when I examine groups that are not my own and that I know less well?

- How willing am I to reexamine my generalizations, to consider contrary evidence, to study the causes of evidence, and to reformulate understandings accordingly?
- To what extent do I challenge the bias of my self-knowledge and consider how this can distort my knowledge of others?
- Do my claimed good intentions exempt me from responsibility for the harmful consequences of my deeds?
- Am I as respectful of the individuality of others as I expect others to be of my individuality?

How we position ourselves relative to these questions of knowing will largely shape the path of racism and prejudice in our society – its persistence or its diminished place in our relationships with each other. There may be no greater challenge in our human interactions than to find and strengthen paths of insight and trust with those whose faces and voices are different than our own.

If we position ourselves in patterns of knowing that make it possible to contest racist and prejudicial perspectives, then values can make a significant difference. If we don't, values are nearly irrelevant or mostly relevant to deceive or mislead. Values that contest racism and prejudice can come from many sources. I'd like to mention two – one universal and another parochial. They are the Golden Rule and a keystone of American culture, the ideal of a "free individual." "Do unto others as you would have them do unto you" is as close to a universal ethical principle as can be found. It is embraced by virtually every religious, wisdom and ethical tradition. The foundation for ethical behavior, it suggests, is self-knowledge.

How do *you* want to be treated? How do *you* want to be understood? Who do *you* want to be in the eyes of others? Do *you* want to be misunderstood and treated as an undifferentiated member of a category – white male or black female? Or do *you* want to be understood and treated as a unique person – Bob or Alice? Do *you* want to be seen in terms of how you live your life or as a stereotype that has no necessary relationship to who you are or how you live? How *you* answer these questions for yourself tells you how you should understand and behave toward others. If *you* want to be a respected person, then the Golden Rule says don't treat others as a disrespected category.

Nothing is a more fundamental denial of America's rhetorical commitment to the "free individual" than racism and prejudice. Painfully, we have an overabundance of overt and covert racism and prejudice in America that comes from people who aggressively shout the claims of individual liberty but live in self-imposed chains. Racism and prejudice are the stubborn refusal to treat others as individuals to say nothing about "free" individuals. Protecting the status of individuals can never be about my individualism and the hell with yours. Our standing as individuals is only as strong as the standing we give to any and all individuals.

Our commitment to liberty is not defined by how much freedom we claim for ourselves but how much we give to others, especially to those we don't understand, agree with or like. Otherwise, we are not "free individuals", but either members of privileged groups living off of arbitrary benefits at the expense of those we don't permit to be free individuals, or members of exploited groups used to give others a false sense of freedom and a perverted individualism.

While it may be true that our lives could not function without generalizations, it is equally true that our generalizations cannot be used to erase the uniqueness of each of us as a specific person. It may be true that the role of generalizations introduces the possibilities of racism and prejudice, but it is equally true that generalizations must be checked to not destroy the uniqueness we experience and claim for ourselves.

Ironically, the most comprehensive generalization of all, that we are all human beings, protects our particularity most securely. As humans, each and every one of us is a unique person with intrinsic value within our own life story.

Still, we must never forget that racism and prejudice are embedded in the legal and structural elements of our political, economic, and social life. It has been necessary, and continues to be necessary, to combat those impediments through relentless efforts for legal and structural changes. Undoing the Constitutional protection for segregation that was provided by <u>Plessy v. Ferguson</u>, undoing the social and economic distortions created by life lived in separate categories defined by race, undoing the racially defined and applied restrictions on voting and the denial of full political participation for all citizens requires committed, unrelenting efforts for new Constitutional standards, Civil Rights legislation, and Voting Rights protections.

Unfortunately, these efforts continue to be as essential today as they were in the 1960s. Consider only one example, the 1965 Voting Rights Act. This legislation provided for the enfranchisement of racial minorities not by creating new rights, but by insuring the implementation of rights provided by the 14th and 15th Amendments to the Constitution in the 19th Century. These were Constitutional rights that were systematically denied because of racism and prejudicial bigotry.

Yet, in 2013, the Supreme Court, in Shelby County v. Holder, made the provisions of the Voting Rights Act unenforceable and we have seen nothing but an aggressive series of efforts to limit the effective participation of those whose rights had been most protected by the act. Shamefully, the Republican Party has built a strategy of gerrymandering and voter suppression to build a power base unrepresentative of the American people. To add insult to injury, the elimination of these protections was the work of phony "originalists" who claimed there was no Constitutional basis for federal supervision of state electoral responsibilities even though Section 2 of the 14th Amendment authorizes Congress to impose even more radical punishments on states for denying the free exercise of franchise rights for all citizens than any punishment available under the voided legislation.

The sustained pursuit of equitable legal and structural standards and operating conditions will always be necessary to limit the detrimental impacts of racism and prejudice. That work will always be necessary, but it will never be sufficient. The generating source of racism and prejudice is not the government or social constructs but you and I as individual human beings and citizens. We not only need to monitor, limit, and guide the structural forms of our world, we need to work relentlessly on ourselves – our attitudes, our understandings, and our behaviors.

We need to create and refresh a sense of *"Transformation"*. Even if we are relatively successful in restraining racism and prejudice in formal, overt components of life, they will remain alive – controlled but secretly virulent – in the private formation of who we are and how we see each other.

I don't believe that matters of race and prejudice present us with the luxury of a binary choice – to be racist or non-racist or to be prejudiced or non-prejudiced. The seeds of racism and prejudice are in us all. The possibilities to limit and transcend racism and prejudice are in us all. The choice is largely in our hands. Do we submit to the drift and constraints of our nature, or do we actively commit ourselves to the transformations that are necessary to move beyond unexamined habits and the natural ironies that make it all too easy to be small, petty, shriveled, and hateful.

Nonviolent Civil Disobedience

Dr. King's strategy and principled commitment to nonviolent civil disobedience has become a cornerstone of my life. It works and it does so on honorable moral grounds. It is both complex and simple. It asks much of us and gives much back to us personally and as a people.

First, it acknowledges and respects the rule of law. There are consequences for violating the law. Those consequences are expected and must be accepted. The goal is not to institute lawlessness but to transform the law. To transform the law, it is necessary to respect the principle of law.

Second, there are standards higher than the law; justice and truth, for example. Those standards need to guide us, but they should be used to transform civil order not to abandon us to chaos or the arbitrariness of brute personal power.

Third, resistance is a necessary component of committed loyalty and membership. Our intense commitment to our children requires us to resist and counter behaviors that are detrimental to their wellbeing. Our love of country is no different. It is not patriotic to accept and endorse anything just because we wrap it in the flag or because it's part of our cultural habits or because in 1896, 2008, or 2013 the Supreme Court said it was Constitutional. That is blindness and mindless, and often hypocritical. When we have failed to be guided by our highest standards, resistance is the noblest form of patriotism.

Fourth, resistance must, itself, be framed by restraint and discipline. The waywardness of our children does not justify abuse. The waywardness of our nation does not justify violence against our people. Nonviolent resistance is the necessary standard for civil transformations in the legal and cultural fabric our nation.

Perhaps the most common and most unworthy so-called moral standard, is retribution – a proverbial eye for an eye. In fact, it requires no moral discipline at all. It is instinctual. It is an impulse, not a moral choice. It defines morality by immortality – I violate you, which then authorizes you to replicate the violation. And, in practice, it almost never is exercised with the restraint of just an eye for an eye. It is almost always, some version of you punched me so I'll beat you up; or you insulted me so I'll destroy your family; or you killed two of our soldiers so we'll kill hundreds of your soldiers and may include some civilian women and children (too bad). Retribution is a principle of immorality.

Nonviolent civil disobedience requires the strength and discipline to go under to overcome. It is something Christians should understand but few do even though their savior died to defeat death and gain eternal life.. It pursues change from a position of overt vulnerability. Transformations from nonviolent civil disobedience are not the product of bullying, of personal impositions of power, of impulsive revenge, of convenience or expediency, or of arbitrary privileges and leverage. They are the product of sacrifice, suffering, and principled purposes.

As an administrator, I learned that my greatest accomplishments were almost always gained when I pursued worthy objectives from a position of vulnerability, not imposition. What many regard as weakness can be strength when pursued with disciplined purpose.

I am a very poor forecaster. For example, in 1997 I confidently predicted that cell phones were a fleeting fad that would soon become nothing more than an oddity. But I can say that IF in 2020 the current administration is given four more years to govern, I will do everything in my power to find every possible opportunity to express nonviolent civil disobedience. I lament that we don't have Dr. King's leadership.

The Public and the Private

Perhaps the most definitive change between the 1960s and 2020 relates to the positioning of the "public" and the "private" in shaping our life as a people. President Kennedy's call to the American people in his inaugural address has become trivialized, unintelligible, or aggressively opposed. Today, the appeal would more likely be the opposite – "ask not what you can do for your country – ask what your country can do for you."

Public service is no longer relevant to political leadership. Civic action is inadequately understood, much less practiced. The common good rarely extends beyond those who want what we want. Compromise, accommodation, tolerance and civility are ridiculed as forms of weakness and unworthiness. Education has been captured by a user fee mentality rather than pursued as investments in building the competencies of a democratic society. Protecting private incomes routinely pushes aside public goods and purposes. And social justice has no compelling place in a world in which only "me" matters.

Not just as Americans, but as human beings, we need a healthy balance between the prerogatives we retain as individual citizens, the private, and the responsibilities we owe to the communities of which we are a part, the public. We have discrete identities that must be respected and we survive only because, from the moment we are born, we are protected, nourished, and able to flourish within the shared life of families, neighborhoods, and nations. We are unique, private persons profoundly woven into public, social webs.

Both our private, personal life and our public, shared life need to be honored. Both need to be related to each other in ways in which the public gives space and vitality to the private as does the private to the public. We have the largest military engine the world has ever known but we express no public purpose to support it, only private incentives for individuals to "volunteer." Any sense of a covenanted people with a common purpose and bond has been transformed into contractual relationships that make us feel that we give up more than we get. Pathetically, at patriotic events, sporting events, and political events we typically portray ourselves as exactly what we are not – a bonded people of common purpose.

The lack of a healthy, positive balance between the public and the private invites two paths to totalitarian tyranny. The one path is what happens when we exaggerate the public and diminish the private. Americans tend to be quite sensitive to this form when they look at the former Soviet Union and China. Some Americans still haven't been blinded to seeing it when they look at contemporary Russia.

The other path is what happens when we exaggerate the private and diminish the public. Americans have considerably more difficulty seeing this, especially in themselves, but it is every bit as sure a path to totalitarian tyranny. The more that personal power is an end in itself and the personal exercise of power (that is, the private) is permitted and protected, the more there will be tyrannical conditions that can lead to results identical to anything created by Stalin, Castro, Mao, and Putin.

When we respect the intrinsic necessity of both private and public spheres and balance them in ways that they both check and enhance each other, we protect ourselves from tyranny and contribute to the vibrant possibilities of liberty. The rule of law, equal opportunity, rigorous 1st Amendment liberties, the equal protection of the rights of citizenship and participation for all, and due process are examples of balancing principles. They are not principles of favoritism. They are abstract, impersonal standards that create a public realm in which each of us has the opportunity to thrive as an individual.

Perhaps the greatest specific loss we have suffered as a people from the disparagement of public life and public responsibilities is a commitment to social justice. A commitment to social justice requires an appreciation and affirmation of our responsibilities to each other as a people. Yes, problems and issues of social justice are impacted by personal choices, behaviors and values. But they will never be resolved or reduced by private choices alone. They are public. They are structural. They are cultural. They are historical. They are imposed. And they will only be meaningfully engaged when we understand that the personal life we cherish is formed within a public life we share.

Misunderstandings

My 1960s experiences in the South not only created new understandings and sensitivities; they also created unfortunate misunderstandings. That, in itself, has been an invaluable learning opportunity for me. For example, I developed a mistaken mind-set that transformed the injustices suffered by blacks into black virtue. Eventually, I realized, the virtue of black people is a positive accomplishment of black people. It is not a consequence of the moral failures, injustices, and crimes of others against them. It is an expectation of moral responsibility from which no one is exempt regardless of the injustices they have suffered and continue to suffer. Virtue is an accomplishment; even more impressive for African Americans living in our society because of the injustices of their history and the persistent injustices that damage and distort their day to day lives. Furthermore, racism is not an injustice only when the victims are virtuous. Racism is always unjust regardless of the moral standing of its victims. It is intrinsically unjust and must be resisted as such.

Another misunderstanding I carried away from these experiences related to my hatred for the south. As a non-southerner, it was too easy for me to isolate the sources of these injustices into a context that was "other" and not my own. I was angry and unforgiving. Southerners seemed to be evil and unredeemable. Over time, I learned to see my relationship with the south through a more complex set of lenses. Returning to the north with fresh eyes quickly showed me that the injustices of the south were not the monopoly of the south. Specific manifestations often varied, but the poison that fed them came from the same vile bottle – north, south, east, or west.

Also, in time, I felt a disorienting attachment to the south, even wanting to return. I think this is partly why I prematurely accepted a job in Texas in 1973. This confused me, but now it seems obvious to me. It is a violation of ourselves whenever we simply reject and hate anything or anyone that has been formative to who we are and what we value about ourselves. My experiences in the south transformed my life. They made me a stronger and better person. They helped me cope with challenges I brought with me. Eventually, I learned the simple truth that hatred and alienation are inadequate responses to components of our lives that have made us who we are, and that have brought into our lives some of what has most contributed to our growth and strength and decency.

Political Correctness

The struggle for social justice has been hampered by a new form of censorship brought to life since the struggles of the 1960s. This censorship is a form of silencing simply by labeling something as "PC" or "politically correct".

Although "PC" is used in a variety of ways, most commonly it is pejorative, and is most frequently applied to language, actions, or policies that support diversity, multiculturalism, affirmative action, opposition to hate speech, tolerance, civility, positions supportive of individuals and groups such as women, minorities, and LGBTQ, and, more recently, issues associated with science such as second-hand smoking, immunizations, HIV/AIDS, and climate change. Interestingly, every target for "PC" labeling can be challenged and opposed without using the label. However, "PC" labeling has a very consistent and powerful roll in current public discourse; a roll that is valued for its effectiveness by those who use it. It is an implicit, but potent, form of censorship. Label anything "PC" and the immediate consequence is to dismiss it, to take it out of the conversation, to diminish its authenticity, or to make it irrelevant or beside the point. A consistent set of perspectives essential to social justice get set aside not by valid and effective argumentation, but by labeling.

I happen to be deeply committed to the honoring and protecting of America's racial and ethnic diversity, for example. I am prepared to defend that commitment. When all I get from those who oppose my view is a "PC" label, I am dismissed without a single shred of considered or meritorious argumentation against me. That is no different than being black balled, and that can never be the basis for the open dialogue essential to a free society.

When Donald Trump calls women, as he has, "fat pigs", "dogs", "slobs", "animals", and "bimbos", claiming that

Megyn Kelly has "…blood coming out of her eyes, blood coming out of her – wherever", I want to contest what he has said, not censor it as "politically incorrect." I don't want to suppress it; I want to challenge it.

Yet the core of Trump's defense is that the country has a problem with "being politically correct." In other words, label those with opposing views into a category of irrelevance and proceed uncontested with his abuses.

As disgusting as Trump is to me, I will defend and protect his opportunities to express himself as he chooses. I will not, however, grant to him and to millions of others like him the opportunity to silence me and relegate me to a category of inauthenticity and irrelevance simply by stamping a label on my commitments.

Faith and Social Justice

My faith informed my life in the south. My life in the south transformed my faith. I was raised in a white Christian home. Although I am not now a Christian, the basis of my separation from the faith is because of a fundamental

disconnection between the theological structure of
Christianity and my understanding of human meaning and
the integrity of human life.

What do I mean? I grew up in a home that captured the
quandary of my life as a Christian. My mother was
Lutheran. My father was Calvinist. Both were embedded in
the unique focus of their respective traditions. Salvation
through faith alone – not works – was the center of my
mother's faith. The responsibilities of hard work and
faithful service anchored my father. I was torn. On the one
hand, I never imagined that I could justify myself before
God and have always felt that the presumption of self-
righteousness was a fundamental flaw. On the other hand,
how I lived my life, especially in my relationships with
others, was the only genuine evidence of my devotion. The
shorthand version of this became – was being a Christian
about my eternal salvation or about my humanity and its
moral responsibilities.

My experiences in the south pushed me away from *sole fide*
salvation. I was compelled to engage the world – to work
for its improvement – not to escape from it to save my
hide.

Further, not only were Christians and their institutionalized forms hypocritical, they were actively evil. I do not believe that religion, in general, or Christianity, in particular, has made our world a better place. I do believe, both then and now, that it has deepened the world's pain and suffering. Yes, there are noble and inspiring men and women of faith, but the balance sheet is dominated by self-righteousness, and every imaginable form of absolutizing what is actually relative. Nothing damages humanity more or more grotesquely distorts the authentic character of our humanity than to claim qualities we don't and won't ever possess.

My essential decision was to live within my best understanding of human life on earth and not to permit myself to be side-tracked and misled by claims beyond my capacity that too often violated and alienated me from my most honorable, even if limited and imperfect, possibilities.

It's my view that life doesn't come to us wrapped up in pre-formed or other-defined meaningfulness. And we are not here to be saved from life; we are here to live fully and responsibly the rare and precious existence we have been given! The glory of human life is the extraordinary opportunity each of us has to create our own meaningful existence – one that gives us purpose and direction and an authentic sense that the infinitesimal speck of time and space we occupy actually does matter.

Recently my daughter asked me about the distinction between an agnostic and an atheist. My feeble, brief response may be helpful in reflecting my personal mindset, even if it is inadequate to more nuanced views.

"For me, an 'agnostic' is someone who simply claims not to know. A 'theist' describes a particular understanding of god; specifically, a notion of god as a transcendent being - a power greater than and beyond this world who is responsible for the destiny of this world. To be precise, an 'atheist' is someone who does not accept or embrace a theistic understanding of god. I am both an agnostic and an atheist. That is, I do not know whether there is something that could be sensibly called a god or not, whatever the form of that god may be – theistic, deistic, or pantheistic. But to simply call myself an agnostic is, for me, a coward's way out. When the question of who I am on the matter of god comes up, to simply say 'I don't know' is a dodge. I am an atheist because I live my life and make sense of my existence without regard to any belief or assumption about a transcendent god or about any other religious teaching or claim based on the reality of such a being.

That is the truth about me and who I am. It does not mean that I know or understand ultimate truths about these matters. I don't. It just means this is the truth about me and how I live this precious existence that is mine. So, yes, I am an agnostic in terms of ultimate knowledge, but I am an atheist in terms of the truth of how I live my mortal existence."

This does not mean that there are not lessons and perspectives I learned in my Christian home that I still respect and struggle to honor and protect today as I did in the 1960s. But it does mean that they do not require a necessary theistic affirmation to be relevant guides to those of us who are searching for a moral center to the only life we know we will have.

I know that Christianity grants no special privileges or protections for America. It doesn't promise secure borders or more jobs or lower taxes or better trade deals or being "great" ever (much less again), or, even, competent and decent leaders. In fact, the Christian Bible neglects to even mention America. I know that Christianity makes no public policies, requires no political parties, offers no political orientation, and endorses no political system relevant to our

relationship with what is true and authentic. I know that
obeying the word of scripture promises only one thing –
salvation in another world; not less obligation to the
Constitution or more obligation to majoritarian preferences.
I know that the only passage in Christian scripture that
relates to taxes (Romans 13:6ff) tells Christians to pay them
with respect. I know that the dangers Christian scripture
most warn us against are wealth and power, license and self-
righteousness. Oh, and by the way, I also know that
most human biological conceptions terminated before birth
are "acts of God," not choices of women.

Most of all, in my Christian home I learned that God loves
everyone and that means I am not exempt from the same
inclusive obligation. I may, actually will, fail to love
inclusively, but it is a failure I must struggle to rectify not
justify. I learned that Jesus' teaching of the two great
commandments did not come with an asterisk that had a
long list of exceptions – love the Lord your God and love
your neighbor as yourself (Matthew 23:37).

I learned that in God's eyes what I do for the *least* among us
is the truest reflection of what I do for God (Matthew
25:40). And I learned that if I hate my brethren who I have
seen I cannot love God who I have not seen (I John 4:20).

In short, I was taught in so many different ways that how I respect my fellow human beings is the truest reflection of devotion to God, or, in my case, authentic humanism..

These are not esoteric teachings hidden in secret texts that require mumbo jumbo interpretations – what my granddaughter calls "magical sky spray". Nor are they scholarly interpretations of obscure passages relevant only to ivory-tower intellectuals. This is not "political correctness" that can be smugly censored simply because it is decent. This is, for Christians, a straightforward reading of what their holy book teaches them.

Over and over, these same teachings are brought to the attention of the faithful. Somehow, they have been translated into unintelligible forms in a large segment of white Christian homes in America today. That Donald Trump is embraced at all, but with such enthusiasm and pride, by so many white American Christians is a betrayal. It is not a political betrayal, but a betrayal of their professed faith. And they, no Muslim, no Jew, no secular humanist, and no atheist, bear the responsibility for that betrayal.

Nevertheless, their betrayal has consequences that have severely damaged the lives of millions and compromised social justice in our society. While they are responsible for the betrayal of their faith, it is the *least* among them who bear the crippling burdens of the consequences of their betrayal. That is the very essence of social injustice.

The Audacity of Hope

It is shameful of me to preempt President Obama's voice. Alternatively, it is an expression of respect to suggest that President Obama, Dr. King, Dr. Francis, Betty Reynolds, and countless others have given me a measure of steadfastness to understand that our hopes, our commitments, and our hard work cannot be defined by single points in time. The "arc of history" is not defined by November 8, 2016 any more than it was by November 6, 2008. It is defined by our audacious insistence to persist and prevail.

While our hope is not defined by a moment in time, we must meet the threats present in the moment. Throughout the intervening 50 years since I left Alabama A & M, there have been some great advances, some dimensions of limited progress, some new challenges, and some diseases that we have been unable to heal or contain. The tilt of those mixed accomplishments, I believe, was in a more hopeful direction. But with a suddenness that could unanchor us, the tilt has reversed and today the forces and voices that defined the resistance to social justice in the 1960s are re-creating their twisted social order. We must meet the challenges of 2020 with the same clarity, steadfastness of commitment, and common purpose as we did more than 50 years ago. That is our audacious hope.

Robert W. Hoffert

CHAPER 8
Sadly, 50 Years Ago Feels Too Much Like Today

On November 8, 2016 Americans elected a long-lived man
who provides not a single credible piece of evidence that he
has ever been committed to anything other than himself and
his transient pleasures to lead our government and represent
our people.

The person who represents me as an American is
incompetent, abusive, criminal, and a traitor. I am not
distressed because his victory was a political defeat. There
already have been many of those in my life. I don't like
them, but I understand that I must accept and deal with
them. Instead, I experienced this as a repudiation of human
decency and a rejection of everything I treasure and struggle
to strengthen about being an American.

I believe that when we have been "great" we offer a refuge,
not rejections; that we extend warm invitations, not build
cold walls; that we are collaborative, not bullies; that we
protect each other, not anoint only our own as worthy of

our embrace; that we trust the decency of each other, not the impulses of a narcissistic megalomaniac.

Since the late 60s there has been a mixture of progress, stagnation, and regression on a variety of fronts impacting social justice for all Americans. Unfortunately, the trends now have become profoundly threatening and dangerous. To say that we are on a regressive path is a kind, but irresponsible, understatement. Whatever progress was made during the intervening decades has been thoughtlessly and purposefully put at risk. This is why President Obama's victory was so important for America. It was not just a victory of party, political orientation, or policy preferences. It was the victory that made a second generation of national regeneration possible. Once again, we could access hopes that challenge our indifference, fears, suspicions, and hatreds. Once again, we could believe in the struggle that supports our best qualities and most noble possibilities. Realistically, that's the struggle we fought to bring to life fifty years ago as well.

I can't exaggerate the pain created by the almost instant dashing of those hopes. Self-proclaimed "fiscally responsible" leaders created a distracting economic emergency that preempted attention to the broader scope of issues essential for social justice progress. Self-proclaimed "birthers" manufactured vacuous claims for no purpose other than to delegitimize the leadership of a decent and competent man. Self-proclaimed "originalists" generated radical departures from Constitutional origins and deep-rooted norms that intensified the abuses of guns and violence, that manipulated the courts and the justice system, that gave money the standing of persons, and that deepened the impediments to voting and full civil protections for our nation's most vulnerable citizens. And self-proclaimed men and women of "principle and character" were unable to commit themselves to any purpose higher than to deny and defeat an honorable, competent, and balanced leader whose greatest offense was the color of his skin. It felt like the reincarnation of the mid-1960s.

But the power of hope is greatest and most needed in the face of hopelessness. I have become an old man. I've been fortunate to have had a rewarding and satisfying life. I grew into my early maturity in an ethos of hope and bountiful opportunities. Even the challenges of civil rights and Vietnam brought purposeful struggles into my life that strengthened me and my resolve to contribute to the building of a better world. My family has filled my emptiness and transformed my life from being trapped to being embraced. And I have celebrated the expression of my humanity as an American. I can easily live out my remaining days within the comforting shadows and echoes of a past that strengthened me and that I cherish..

But I cannot assume that promising possibilities will still be true for the principles and purposes for which I lived and within which my life was enriched. I cannot assume they will be true for my daughters, for my four grandchildren, for the family and dear friends I most cherish, or for the millions who live under conditions that diminish and damage them due to nothing that was in their control. And I cannot assume they will remain true for this place on earth, America, that has given me direction, a home, and my cultural identity.

The current president, his administration, almost all Congressional Republicans, and those among us who supported and continue to support them are attacking the foundation of an honorable world and a nation that has struggled toward greater justice for all. I have no intention to give them the benefit of my silent acquiescence. I don't ask that you agree with me. I do ask that you consider giving your voice of affirmation to help us to regain the primacy of a path of civil decency and social justice.

Let me, first, make it clear what is **not** the basis of my current distress. My deep concerns are not about party identification, political orientation, or, even, policy preferences. Those are matters about which all of us have had and will continue to have disagreements and differences. At times, it may be hard to swallow, but that is as it should be in a democratic society.

The distress I am expressing is **not** related to party, even though that is distressing. In a broad historical perspective, I view the Republican Party as one with an honorable political tradition that made many valuable contributions to American life. In more recent times, however, it is a party that has sold its birthright. In the name of "tradition," it has turned against its own heritage and trashed it. While sad, that is their problem; not mine. I'm perfectly willing to hold them accountable for the consequences of their betrayal, but it's their burden to carry.

While my sympathy with the contemporary Democratic Party has been grounded in its greater awareness and responsiveness to the voices and needs of all citizens, its timid, apologetic, and, too often, muted affirmation of the positive principles that benefit all Americans has, frankly, disgusted me. When you permit yourself to be silenced by the censorship of "political correctness," you also have betrayed your birthright.

If my only choice is to be a Republican or a Democrat, I am a Democrat, if for no other reason than that it retains some capacity to affirm that every citizen's claim should have equal standing. My preference would be to be neither and to find a new home in a multi-party system. By the way, I believe there is a simple and direct path to a multi-party system in America. Ask me!

The distress I write about is **not** related to political orientation or philosophy, even though that too is distressing. We've been patterned into meaningless chatter about "conservatives" and "liberals". It's chatter that lacks rigorous historical or conceptual coherence. Although most who know me, presume that I'm some kind of liberal, I think of myself as a syncretistic Burkean conservative. In a world of garbled and arbitrary categories, it's easier to just avoid labels of any kind. We have so-called "conservatives" who trash their own tradition and so-called "liberals" who are apologetic or hesitant to explain and defend the tenants of their own tradition. In short, we are overwhelmed by so-called liberals and so-called conservatives whose greatest accomplishment is to misrepresent and discredit the best of their own heritages.

The distress I am writing about is **not** related to policy choices, even though they are distressing. Long before Trump and long after Trump, as well, we will have deep policy differences with each other. It may not seem this way, but, depending on how we handle those differences, they could be beneficial to us as a people in the long run. We benefit more from integrating a variety of perspectives than from imposing a single vision. My policy preferences are sharply different than those of the current administration, but they are rooted in differences among us as a people and would have been just as real if a different administration was now governing.

Trump didn't create the notion that we are "great" when we isolate ourselves and bully others. He just gave it a voice.

Trump didn't create the notion that jobs, convenience, and profit negate efforts to achieve greater environmental responsibility. He just gave it a voice.

Trump didn't create the notion that those who look, and speak, and draw on traditions of meaning different than current American majoritarian norms are, correspondingly, unworthy and dangerous. He just gave it a voice.

Trump didn't create the appeal of banning Muslims from countries that have been the source of no attacks against us while snuggling up with Saudis who have been the overwhelming source of those attacks. He just gave outlets for unconsidered bias.

Trump certainly didn't transform the most assertive and mobilized expressions of American Christianity from an affirmation of universal love for all, including the most despised and rejected, into a form of selectively modified Leviticus legalism. He just gave it a voice.

Trump didn't give birth to virulent or subtly disdaining attitudes toward women, racial or cultural groups, gender and sexual differences, or non-Christian faith and meaning traditions. He just gave it a voice.

Trump is not the first American politician, and will not be the last, to convince the least among us to protect the interests of those with the most while putting themselves at risk. He just created a mass passion for masochism.

Trump didn't dream up schemes to reduce access to the full and equal participation and impact of all citizens. He just reaped its fruit.

Trump didn't originate single-issue thinking and voting whose unintended consequences almost always create betrayal in the long run. He just knew how to exploit it.

Trump didn't manufacture the cruel indifference to 57% of all American families who are unable to come up with $500 to meet immediate emergencies. He already possessed that indifference.

Trump didn't dream up the ideas of building walls of privilege rather than doors of opportunity. He cashed in on those visions.

All of this exists with or without Trump. It exists because it's in us. It reflects us and our differences with each other. Just as he didn't create the policy conflicts among us, he will not resolve them. If they are resolved, intensified, or moderated, it will be because of us.

When I permit myself to move from my momentary impulses to more broadly framed reflections, I understand that this is as it will be in a democratic society of free citizens. We can't simultaneously give each other liberty and then presume to determine the conclusions that our "freedom" requires us to reach.

Although I'm often deeply distressed, I need to live and work within the challenges liberty creates. Ultimately, my commitment to liberty is not measured by how much freedom I want for myself, but how much freedom I am willing to protect for those who are most disagreeable to me.

What does distress me and what does require the fullness of my energy to resist are the following.

- The foundation of factual reliability is being systematically and purposefully destroyed.
- There is a selective indifference to precedence and the norms that have charted paths to greater justice. Long established norms of restraint, precedence, decency, fairness, political independence, loyal opposition, and limits on personal power are being trashed—trashed by a leader and a party that shamelessly calls itself "conservative" as they uproot the past and jeopardize the future.

- Double standards have been transformed from failures to be overcome into virtues to be pursued.

- Democratic leadership has shriveled into self-aggrandizement and privileges for those already most advantaged.

- The rule of law has been replaced by the rule of power and will.

- Perhaps everything above is encapsulated in the shocking lack of civility.

At least in some quarters, vulgar crudity has become celebrated as a form of authenticity. We have forgotten that the simple decency of respect for each person's humanity is not based on who we agree with, who we like, who will help us get what we want, or who is like us. It is based on the core principle of the Declaration of Independence – we are all created equal. Obviously, we are not created identically. However, we are equal in the authenticity of every person's worth and standing as a human being.

Today we are led by white men – yes, disproportionately white men -- who have turned their backs on this noble affirmation. When grown men, in the context of seeking a society's highest office, reduce that discourse to penis-size and dismiss criticisms of vulgar language against women, hateful language against Mexicans, intolerant language against Muslims, the language of contempt against homosexuals and transgender persons, and hostile language against those who need the most and have the least as "political correctness", you know we've sunk into a cesspool.

There is nothing admirable about abuse, bullying, or using privileges to diminish others. It requires nothing more than a lack of control over one's unprocessed impulses.

Although the familiar understanding of civility is essential to life in a democratic society and would greatly elevate our life as a people if we could find our way back to something resembling its decency, there is a deeper meaning to civility we need to revitalize. Civility, ultimately, is about the attitudes essential to being a good citizen. It is about civic responsibility. Quite apart from manners, there is nothing responsible or appropriate for democratic citizenship, in crude, hateful, and hurtful ad hominine attacks. And to excuse or ignore them is no better than to express them.

Most fundamentally, the lack of civility in terms of civic purpose and responsibility has created an atmosphere of despair for many. The bullies delight in knowing they have

caused pain. Recently, Michelle Goldberg expressed the antidote. "Left to fester, [despair] can lead to apathy and withdrawal. Channeled properly, it can fuel an uprising."*
It's time to speak, stand, and move.

*Michelle Goldberg, "Democracy Grief is Real", New York Times Online, December 13, 2019.

Robert W. Hoffert

A last word

The 1968 assassinations of Dr. King and Robert Kennedy were tipping points for me, but my experiences in Alabama, as a whole, moved me to a more encased and self-referencing life. Many factors contributed to this process, but the most basic factor, I believe, was that I lived and worked within a contradiction. My work as an educator in Alabama was to serve young women and men in ways that would encourage and support their own efforts to transform their lives. Unfortunately, I did this within an institution and system that was designed and controlled to prevent that from happening in meaningfully autonomous ways. It was immobilizing to work on behalf of students in an institution historically designed to serve them that was being manipulated by others whose only consistent goal was to keep those same students subservient and impaired.

In St. Augustine I joined with inspiring people committed to social justice. At Boggs, I worked with people I admired and who were dedicated to providing educational opportunities for young boys and girls that otherwise were unavailable in their region. Dr. Francis was preeminent among them. There was a different reality in Alabama. There I was working in a State operated institution dedicated to keeping black people in controlled places and compromised positions. The people who ran the university on campus were the interface between aspiring black students and educators hoping for opportunities and transformational impacts and white State officials intent on maintaining structures of subordination. I experienced a continuous struggle between my passion for my students and my quarrels with the ineffectual leadership and their betrayals that kept Governor Wallace happy and protected his racist agenda of bigotry.

Since 1968, my life has been centered on myself – my education, my career, my family. Sometimes I feel sad, sometimes ashamed, but often I lament that I didn't persist on the front line of a struggle for social justice and the nobler spirit of our nation. At the same time, my entire life has been formed within the commitments that brought me to St. Augustine and Boggs and Alabama A and M, and the experiences they brought into my life. Since 1968, I have carried within me these two conflicting realities – a life simultaneously separated from and merged with these formative values and experiences. I've come to realize that both contain truth about the life I have composed. I have lived within the protective cover of my white privileges. And I have lived with a deep commitment to social justice and an imperative to honor the intrinsic value of every human being.

The experiences I shared with you in these writings make it possible for me both to see my self-centered shortcomings and to anchor myself steadfastly in the commitment to create a society of equals that will not waiver from the hard work of actually being who we claim to be – "one nation, indivisible, with liberty and justice for all."

Robert W. Hoffert

Gratitude

It is difficult for civilized homo sapiens to properly express gratitude. We are intrinsically parasitic; it's the consequence of being embedded in human cultures and civilizations. We live off each other. And it is impossible to sort out the threads to which we owe the most. Let me simply say this – I am grateful for my humanity.

I am grateful to the many African Americans who allowed me to share their stories, their suffering, their struggles, and their accomplishments. Students, colleagues, supervisors, friends, and fellow citizens generously made a place for me even as they were denied a place in the world from which I came. I can't begin to name them all, but there are four persons I will always celebrate – Dr. Charles Francis, Betty Reynolds, Dr. Jerry Shipman, and the elderly woman in St. Augustine who gave me shelter, whose name I cannot access, but whose humanity lives gratefully within me.

My parents' love protected and strengthened me. Although they were unschooled, and lived encased within an isolated, parochial world, they implicitly understood that the principles and values they claimed for themselves were the same principles that all others could equally claim.

I imagine I was not an easy sibling. Yet my brother, Dave, even if bewildered by me at times, has always been there for me without hesitation or qualification.

My friend Alex has deepened and expanded the dimensions of social justice to which I have become more self-consciously aware.

I am inspired by the nurturing creativity and social conscience Ryan has brought into the life of our family.

For almost fifty years, Maureen has generously given me her expressions of love and steadfast loyalty even in the face of my stubborn orneriness, failures and limitations, and she helped and encouraged me to become a better father than I ever would have been without her.

Shoshana and Bird have given me an enlarged sense of self that has helped me become more fully human. They are remarkably different, but, ultimately, remarkably similar. Both are tender and tough. Each, in her own way, weaves together empathy and tenacity to be instruments in service to social justice.

For my grandchildren – Graham, Roberta, Reis, and Jake – I must express a lament. I wish I had done more to leave behind a better world for you to live in and to make your contributions.

And I am grateful to Clark Parsons of Jujapa Press, LLC, the publisher of this book. He was not only consistently responsive and competent in moving through the process; he has created a remarkable approach to broadening and enabling the sharing of human expression.

Robert W. Hoffert

www.ingramcontent.com/pod-product-compliance
Lightning Source LLC
Chambersburg PA
CBHW050734030426
42336CB00012B/1554